100 Años | BRAND

The second most popular tequila in Mexico, the 100 Años line includes blanco, reposado and añejo expressions that, depending on the market, are either 100 percent agave or mixto tequilas. 100 Años is produced in the Mexican lowlands at NOM 1102 in the town of Tequila. All 100 Años tequilas begin by extracting inulin from blue agave piñas with a diffuser. The resulting liquid is then pumped into large autoclaves that use heat and high pressure to cook (hydrolyse) the inulin into fermentable sugars. These agave sugars are pumped into fermentation tanks and either fermented on their own for 100 percent agave tequilas or mixed with cane sugar to make 51 percent agave mixto tequilas. All 100 Años tequilas are then column distilled before being proofed for the blanco expression or barrelled for any of the aged expressions. 100 Años is owned by international spirits conglomerate Beam Suntory, so it is quite likely that the reposado and añejo expressions are matured in ex-bourbon barrels from Jim Beam before being bottled.

100 percent agave | CLASSIFICATION

A labelling term that is regulated by the Mexican government. Tequilas made from a ferment

of 100 percent agave sugars are allowed to add the terms "100% agave", "100% de agave", "100% puro de agave" or "100% puro agave" to their labels. For a long time, this was a marker of quality that could distinguish traditional tequilas from mixto tequilas that were distilled from a wash containing only 51 percent agave sugars. However, since the introduction of the diffuser in tequila production – which extracts agave sugars without cooking the piñas – the 100 percent agave label is not as strong as it once was. Diffusers are much more efficient in extracting agave sugars, which lowers the cost of production, although there is a cost in terms of the flavour and aromas produced during fermentation. In the community of tequila aficionados, there is a growing consensus that diffuser tequilas do not taste as good as those that use brick ovens or even autoclaves. Lastly, mezcals can also add the term "100% agave" or "100% maguey" but, because mixto mezcal is not legally allowed, all certified mezcals are known to be made from 100 percent agave, regardless.

1800 Tequila | BRAND

SEE ALSO
Brick oven p49
French oak p108
Jose Cuervo p138
Normas Oficiales Mexicanas (NOM) p171
White oak p241

Among the top five bestselling tequilas in the USA, 1800 Tequila is produced at Casa Cuervo, NOM 1122, which is owned by the Beckmann family, descendants of Don Jose Antonio de Cuervo. The name 1800 refers to the year Casa Cuervo claims tequila was first aged in oak barrels. First released in 1975 as a premium tequila, 1800 comes in silver, reposado and añejo expressions made from 100 percent blue agave. According to Casa Cuervo, it harvests mature blue agaves between eight and twelve years old. The piñas are halved and steam-cooked in brick ovens for 48 hours before the agave is milled to collect the liquefied sugars. The agave juice is pumped into 50,000-litre (about 13,200gal [US]) fermenters for about 50 hours. When fermentation has finished the agave wine is double distilled. Some of the unaged spirit is used for bottling the silver expression, and the rest of the spirit goes into oak barrels. The reposado spends six months in French and American white oak, while the añejo spends fourteen months in just French oak.

Abocado (mellowing) | PRODUCTION

Mexican regulations allow tequila and sotol to be mellowed with the addition of caramel colour, oak extract, glycerine and/or sugar syrup. Abocado, or mellowing, allows a distiller to soften a spirit and add colour and character to it without the time and expense of maturing it in a wooden barrel. Caramel colouring can be added to unaged spirits to give it a golden colour, or it can be added to batches of reposado or añejo spirits to standardize the colour from multiple barrels before bottling. Oak extract can add both colour and wood character, while glycerine and sugar syrup add softness and sweetness to the spirit and can reduce any harshness from the alcohol.

ABV

See "Alcohol by volume (ABV)" (page 25).

Agave (maguey) | PLANT

A genus (*Agave* spp.) of flowering plants native to Mexico, although they can be found growing anywhere from the American Southwest to northern South America. Agaves are succulents

with a large rosette of thick, fleshy and spiny leaves. Agaves store energy in the form of a soluble fibre called inulin and, depending on the species, can take from five to thirty years to become sexually mature. In general, agaves have two reproductive strategies: one, to create cloned offshoots at the base of the mother plant; and two, to flower and seed. Agaves are also monocarpic plants, meaning that they flower only once in their life cycle, spreading their seeds and then dying, as opposed to polycarpic plants that flower multiple times in their lifespan. Referred to in Nahuatl as *metl* and in Spanish as *maguey*, agaves have historically been used as a source of food, fibre, needles and alcohol. In the 19th century, agaves were transported to other countries as ornamental plants and taken to South Africa as a reserve food supply for grazing cattle.

Agave syrup | COCKTAIL INGREDIENT

A food sweetener derived from agave plants, most commonly the blue agave (*Agave tequilana* var. azul). On average, blue agave can take six to ten years to mature. Once the agave has reached maturity, harvesters will cut the spiny leaves away from the heart of the plant and detach it from its base. Agaves store their plant energy as inulin, a type of soluble fibre that is non-digestible by humans. However, inulin is water soluble and in the presence of heat can break down into fructose, sucrose and glucose. Because of this, agaves are either cooked with steam, shredded and pressed to collect the sugar-rich water, or raw agaves are shredded, rinsed in hot water to extract the inulin and then that inulin water is heated to convert the inulin into digestible sugars. The result in both processes is a mixture of water and sugars from the agave.

For agave syrups, this mixture is concentrated by reducing the total volume of water, giving the mixture a thicker consistency, somewhere between simple syrup and honey. In the early 2000s, agave sweetener became increasingly popular as a sugar substitute because it was perceived as being natural, it tastes sweeter than regular sugar (which suggested that people might consume fewer calories), and it has a lower glycaemic index (GI) than regular white cane sugar. The glycaemic index measures how quickly a person's blood-sugar level will rise after eating. Agave syrup has a lower glycaemic index because it consists of up to 90 percent fructose compared to cane sugar, which is 50/50 fructose and glucose. Glucose does not need to be processed by the gut or liver before being used by the cells for energy, which is why foods with more glucose raise blood-sugar levels faster. In contrast, fructose must first be processed by the liver, which is why it is slower to raise blood-sugar levels. However, in the 2010s, research began to show that consuming significant levels of fructose can cause liver damage, increase cholesterol and contribute to cardiovascular disease.

Agave tequilana

See "Blue agave" (page 45).

Agavoni | COCKTAIL

Created by the German bartender and drinks writer Bastian Heuser, the Agavoni is a variation of the incredibly flexible combination of spirit, Campari and sweet vermouth. And, according to US spirits writer Paul Clarke, the Agavoni pairs

SEE ALSO
Mezcal Negroni *p159*

the freshness of blanco tequila with the citrus from the Campari to make a drink that tastes like spring.

AGAVONI RECIPE

25 ML / ¾ FL OZ BLANCO TEQUILA
25 ML / ¾ FL OZ CAMPARI
25 ML / ¾ FL OZ SWEET VERMOUTH
2 DASHES ORANGE BITTERS

Fill a mixing glass with ice and add equal parts of blanco tequila, Campari and sweet vermouth with two dashes of orange bitters. Stir to mix, chill and dilute slightly. Strain into an Old Fashioned glass filled with ice and garnish with a grapefruit twist. The drink can also be built in the glass: fill an Old Fashioned glass with ice, add all ingredients, stir to mix and garnish with a grapefruit twist.

Aguardiente | CLASSIFICATION

SEE ALSO
Alcohol by volume (ABV) *p25*
Denomination of Origin for
   Mezcal (DOM) *p80*
Denomination of Origin for
   Tequila (DOT) *p83*

Roughly translated as "firewater", aguardiente is a catch-all term in Mexico for distilled spirits that do not fit into any established category. Mexican law defines aguardiente as any spirit distilled from a fermented mash or wash of any agricultural commodity if that commodity makes up at least 51 percent of the fermentable sugars, and is bottled between 35% and 55% ABV. It is possible to have an aguardiente de caña (sugar cane), frutas (fruit) or agave, among others. The term "aguardiente de agave" is used by the distillers whose spirits either do not conform to the Denomination of Origin (DO) regulations or where spirits are made outside one of the DO zones for agave spirits such as tequila or mezcal.

Alambique (copper pot still) | PRODUCTION

SEE ALSO
Column still *p67*

The alambique (alembic in English) is a pot still traditionally made of copper that was invented around 800 AD by the Arab alchemist Jabir ibn

Hayyan. The Arabs used the alembic to create perfume and herbal concentrates for medicinal purposes. The Muslim conquest of Hispania (the Iberian Peninsula) introduced this technology to Europe, where it was used for both medicine and beverage alcohol. During the 16th-century conquest of Mesoamerica, the Spanish brought the alembic with them and used it to distil spirits from sugar cane, fruits and agave. The alembic still is also referred to as a "pot still" because it is essentially a pot with a top shaped with a narrow opening. As the contents of the still are heated, alcohol evaporates and rises upward. Slowly, the vapours progress through the narrowing head, which leads to thin tubing that is usually surrounded by water to cool the vapours into a liquid that can be collected. Because of its shape, the pot still is effective but less efficient than the more modern column stills. In tequila production, alembic stills can be made of copper or stainless steel; however, the use of copper in distillation is important because it helps to remove sulphur from spirits that might otherwise have an off aroma and flavour.

SEE ALSO
Proofing *p193*

Alcohol by volume (ABV) | PRODUCTION

A measure of the alcohol concentration in a mixture per unit of volume. Alcohol by volume, sometimes abbreviated as either Alc by Vol or ABV, states the percentage of the volume of a mixture, usually an alcoholic beverage, that is made up of pure alcohol. Because alcohol is less dense than water, it is possible to use a hydrometer to measure the density of a liquid and from that determine what proportion of the liquid is alcohol. However, one drawback to measuring alcohol by its volume is that the volume of a given sample also depends on temperature, so when hydrometer readings are taken a second calculation must be done to adjust for temperature. Most manuals giving the relationship between a hydrometer reading and ABV are set at 20 °C (68 °F).

Alembic

See "Alambique" (page 22).

Altos de Jalisco | REGION

A geographic region of the eastern portion of the Mexican state of Jalisco. Los Altos de Jalisco (the Jaliscan Highlands) is the second highest tequila-producing region within the Denomination of Origin (DO) – Los Altos sit between 1,735m and 2,130m (about 5,700–7,000ft) in elevation. With its higher altitude than the Tequila Valley, the climate tends to be cooler and the soil is mostly red clay. The agaves grown in this region tend to take longer to mature because of lower average temperatures and because they grow on hillsides rather than a valley floor. Because of these differences, agaves from this region are described as being sweeter, with more fruit and floral notes that come through in the distillate. Drawing on the success of the wine and Scotch world, it has become more common for tequila distilleries and brands to promote the region that their agaves come from. However, when a panel of experts blind-tasted tequila from Los Altos and the Tequila Valley, the region played no role in their preferences for most tasters. Tapatio, Cazadores and Patrón are among the best-known tequilas from Los Altos.

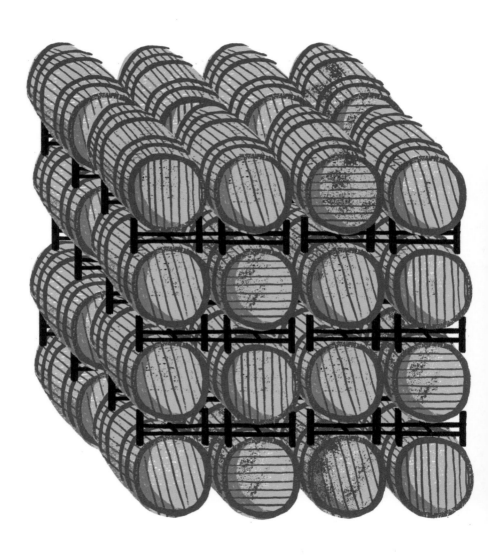

Ana Valenzuela | PEOPLE

A scientist and writer who has been an important voice advocating for the adoption of more sustainable practices in the tequila industry. She is the co-author of the 2004 book *Tequila: A Natural and Cultural History*. In her writing, she warns about the biological dangers of monocropping and the potential for a population crash among cloned blue agave. She has offered strategies that can be adopted by agave growers to strengthen the gene pool for blue agave and create an environment less likely to collapse. Intercropping (planting corn, beans, squash or other types of plants in among blue agave) can slow the spread of pest or disease among the agaves and potentially reduce the amount of chemical fertilizers, pesticides and fungicides used in the plantations. However, intercropping takes space in the field, so it would reduce the number of agaves planted per hectare. One other suggestion is to allow all subspecies of *Agave tequilana* to be used for tequila production. Blue agave is just one of four *A. tequilana* subspecies; adding the remaining three into production would increase the genetic diversity of the plants and help to stave off a crash.

Ancestral mezcal

See "Mezcal ancestral" (page 155).

Añejo | CLASSIFICATION

A regulated labelling term in Mexico as a nonspecific age statement for tequila and mezcal. Añejo tequilas (mixto or 100 percent agave) must spend between one and three years in an oak barrel or container that is no more than

600 litres (almost 160gal [US]) in volume. While añejo translates as "aged" or "old", if a producer chooses to use an English translation of añejo on the label, it must say "extra aged". For mezcal, mezcal artesanal or mezcal ancestral to be labelled añejo, it must spend more than 12 months in a wooden container that is less than 1,000 litres (almost 264gal [US]) and stored in an area with minimal variations in light, temperature and humidity. While the regulation for añejo mezcal requires a wood container, it does not specify that the wood be oak. While, in practice, it is likely that almost all añejo mezcal is stored in oak barrels, this opens the possibility of using other wood sources in a similar way to Brazilian cachaça.

Artisanal mezcal

See "Mezcal artesenal" (page 156).

Autoclave | PRODUCTION

SEE ALSO
Horno *p130*
Piña *p190*

A pressurized vessel that also applies heat to whatever is placed inside. Mexican regulations allow some varieties of agave spirits, such as tequila and mezcal, to use an autoclave to cook the piñas before they are broken down and fermented. The autoclave is filled with whole or halved piñas until it is full. The door is sealed, and the closed system is pressurized with steam heat. While cooking piñas in a traditional horno (earthen pit oven) can take five days, an autoclave can fully cook the piñas in as little as 12 hours depending on the temperature and pressure used. Because of this reduced cooking time, tequila producers can reduce their production costs, which can translate into a lower retail price and/or a higher profit margin.

Avión | BRAND

Founded by Ken Austin in 2010, Avión is sourced from NOM 1416 in the highlands of eastern Jalisco. The piñas are cooked in brick ovens for three days, fermented and then pot-distilled. After distillation the tequila is filtered. Some of the unaged tequila is bottled for the brand's silver expression at 40% ABV and some of the tequila is aged in oak barrels. The reposado is matured for six months and the añejo is matured for two years. Shortly after its launch, Avión signed a global distribution agreement with Pernod Ricard in 2011; and in January 2018, Pernod fully purchased Avión for an undisclosed sum.

B
35

Bacanora | CLASSIFICATION

SEE ALSO
Denomination of Origin for
   Bacanora (DOB) *p79*
Sonora *p214*

A spirit distilled from *Agave angustifolia* Haw.
in the Mexican state of Sonora. While it has been
produced in Sonora in and around the town
of Bacanora for hundreds of years, bacanora
was outlawed from 1915 to 1992. Similarly to
Prohibition in the USA, the criminalization of its
distillation did not stop production but pushed
it underground, into a black market. Seven
years after the ban was lifted the Secretariat
of Economic Development and Productivity of
Sonora requested that bacanora be made legal
and given a Denomination of Origin (DO). In
2000, the DO for bacanora became official and
laid out the rules for production. Bacanora can
be made only from *A. angustifolia*, the same
variety of agave most commonly used to make
mezcal but grown in the DO region for bacanora.
Traditionally, the agave used in Sonora was
referred to as *A. pacifica* or *A. yaquiana* but it was
later discovered that it was in fact not a different
species of agave but simply *A. angustifolia* shaped
by the growing region of the Sonoran highlands.

Bacardi Ltd | BRAND

SEE ALSO
Cazadores *p58*
Normas Oficiales Mexicanas
   (NOM) *p171*
Patrón *p184*

Founded by Don Facundo Bacardí Massó in
Santiago, Cuba, on 4 February 1862, Bacardi

was a one-brand company focused on rum for 130 years. In 1993, Bacardi branched out of the rum business with its purchase of Italy's Martini & Rossi and since then has continued to expand its portfolio, which includes four tequila brands all produced out of NOM 1487 in Los Altos de Jalisco. In addition to Corzo Tequila, Cuatro Vientos and Camino Real, Bacardi owns and markets Cazadores Tequila, which it purchased in 2002. In January 2018, Bacardi announced that it was purchasing Patrón Tequila for a reported $5.1 billion, making Bacardi one of the largest spirit producers in the super-premium tequila-market segment.

SEE ALSO
Vinaza *p239*

Bagasse | BY-PRODUCT

The fibrous material left over from processing sugar cane or agave. In the sugar-making process, the cane is crushed to extract the juice, then used to make sugar. The cane bagasse is used as a biofuel to generate electricity or it can be used to make building materials. Bagasse created during the production of agave spirits has little commercial use without significant processing. However, there are some promising developments. In tequila production, bagasse is used as a biofuel to heat boilers, as a supplemental feed source for sheep, as compost and as a building material. One company is creating pulp from the bagasse that is then converted into compressed fibre board. Similarly, Sombra Mezcal led by Richard Betts has begun a pilot programme to use bagasse and vinaza to create adobe bricks, and it is exploring the use of bagasse as a biofuel to heat its stills.

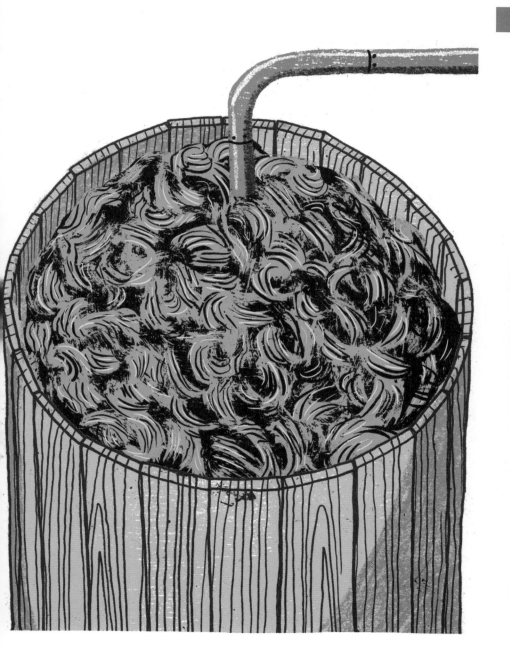

Barrel | PRODUCTION

A wooden vessel used to hold goods. Before containers transformed the world's shipping systems, many goods were stored and transported in wooden barrels. The wood barrel was invented in Northern Europe, where they were used for storing wine as early as the Roman imperial period. Barrel technology quickly spread across Europe, and the positive interaction between wood (oak in particular) and distilled spirits was discovered as a by-product of the need to transport liquids such as brandy, rum and whisky in watertight containers. With this realization, distillers began maturing their spirits in wooden barrels on purpose to soften the spirit as it rested, give it some colour and add wood flavours to it. Mexico, just like the USA and the Caribbean, had a long tradition of drinking its locally made spirits completely unaged. However, as the tequila industry grew and necessitated the transportation of the spirit outside of Jalisco, aged tequila was invented.

Bats | ANIMAL

A flying mammal known for being nocturnal and using echolocation to move about in the world. Despite their popular association with evil, they are very helpful to humans. Some species of bats eat insects that can damage crops, which can help to reduce the total amount of pesticides sprayed on fields and control mosquito populations, for example. Other types of bat get their food from fruit and nectar. These bats are excellent pollinators and in Mexico are one of the primary ways in which agave seeds are pollinated. However, most blue agave plants for tequila are not allowed to bloom and instead are cloned, which negatively impacts the genetic diversity of the plant and removes an important food source for the bats. In 2017, the International Union for Conservation of Nature, Universidad Autónoma de México and the Tequila Interchange Project created a "Bat Friendly" certification for agave spirits. The certification verifies that tequila producers are sourcing their agave from fields that allow 5 percent of their plants to flower and not be harvested for production. This helps both to create genetic diversity in the agaves and to feed the bats that are a threatened species.

Beam Suntory | BRAND

A subsidiary of Suntory Holdings and producers of Jim Beam Bourbon, Beam Suntory formed in 2014 when Suntory of Osaka, Japan, purchased Beam, Inc. for $16 billion, making it the third largest producer of distilled spirits. In 1795, Jacob Beam began distilling and selling corn whiskey. His family ran the company until Prohibition, when it was forced to close. Post-Prohibition, the family reopened the distillery but had to sell after World War II. Through a series of mergers and acquisitions, Fortune Brand purchased both Beam and Sauza Tequila in 2005 and reformed as Beam Global Spirits & Wine, Inc. With this purchase, the new Beam now owned Sauza, 100 Años, Hornitos, Tres Generaciones and El Tesoro tequilas. Meanwhile, in 1899, Shinjirō Torii opened a shop in Osaka to sell imported wine. In 1923, Torii built the Yamazaki Distillery to make Scotch-style whisky in Japan. Over time, Suntory gradually expanded into other Japanese food and beverage categories until its purchase of Beam added a global portfolio of distilled spirits.

SEE ALSO
Autoclave *p30*
Brick oven *p49*

Bitter honey
(*mieles armagas*) | PRODUCTION

The dirty liquid collected and discarded during
the first couple of hours when cooking agave
piñas with steam. Whether a distiller is using a
brick oven or an autoclave, the initial application
of steam heat causes the piñas to sweat, rinsing
any residual dirt, wax or even pesticides off the
agaves. Many ovens and autoclaves contain a
false bottom that allows the *mieles armagas*,
or bitter honey, to collect and then be drained
off so as not to pollute the resulting ferment.
Experienced tequileros attest that, if this step is
not done, then it can produce a spirit that has a
harsh or bitter character to it.

SEE ALSO
Mezcal *p155*
Mezcal ancestral *p155*
Mezcal artesanal *p156*
Mixto *p163*
Tequila *p83*

Blanco | CLASSIFICATION

A regulated labelling term in Mexico for spirits.
For tequila, blanco refers to a mixto or 100
percent agave tequila that is transparent, though
not necessarily colourless, and is only diluted
to bottling strength with water. Also, blanco
tequilas may be matured in oak barrels for less
than two months. Instead of blanco, a producer
may also label their tequila as plata or silver. For
mezcal, any category of the spirit labelled blanco
or joven refers to a mezcal that is colourless
and translucent because it has not been aged or
processed in any way post-distillation except
for reducing the alcohol concentration before
bottling.

SEE ALSO
Lemon *p145*

Bloody Maria | COCKTAIL

A variation of the classic morning cocktail the
Bloody Mary, the Bloody Maria substitutes vodka
with blanco tequila.

BLOODY MARIA RECIPE

60ML / 2FL OZ BLANCO TEQUILA

120ML / 4FL OZ TOMATO JUICE

15ML / ½FL OZ OR 3 TSP LEMON JUICE

4 DASHES WORCESTERSHIRE SAUCE

2 DASHES TABASCO SAUCE

2 DASHES TAPATÍO HOT SAUCE

½ TBSP GRATED HORSERADISH, TO TASTE

1 PINCH CELERY SALT

1 PINCH GROUND BLACK PEPPER

Add all ingredients into a cocktail shaker with ice and shake briefly to mix. Strain into a pint glass filled with ice, and garnish with a lemon wedge and a lime wedge. Feel free to add additional garnishes such as a cucumber spear, pickled vegetables, jalapeño slices or even the Mexican queso fresco ("fresh cheese").

Blue agave (*Agave tequilana*) | PLANT

SEE ALSO
Agave *p16*
Population crash *p190*

Agave tequilana or *A. tequilana* F A C Weber is a species of agave plants native to Western Mexico. The plant was given its binomial taxonomy name by Frédéric Albert Constantin Weber who was a physician on a French military expedition to Mexico of 1864–7. *A. tequilana* is found predominantly in the Mexican state of Jalisco around the town of Tequila from which the plant gets its name. However, *A. tequilana* grows well in several other states, including Nayarit, Guanajuato, Michoacán and Tamaulipas. On average, *A. tequilana* reaches full maturity after five to ten years of growth, at which point the plant will begin the process of flowering at the end of its life cycle. A tall central stalk, called a quiote, shoots up about 5m (16ft) into the air and flowers. Bats, as well as insects and birds, pollinate the seeds, which explode from their pods as the agave is dying. In addition to flowering, *A. tequilana* can also reproduce through cloning. Cuttings of the plant can be taken and regrown, or the agave will sprout new offshoots that are genetic copies of the mother plant. *A. tequilana* has four varieties: azul, azul listado, sigüín and pata de mula. Of these, azul is the best-known and most widely cultivated. By law, tequila producers may use only *A. tequilana* var. azul, also known simply as blue agave, to produce their spirit. Because of the reliance on only one variety of the plant and the widespread use of cloning, blue agave is susceptible to collapse when a pest or disease finds susceptible plants that are all genetically identical.

Boom-and-bust cycle | PRODUCTION

The history of tequila is characterized by a series of boom-and-bust cycles. Some of these were caused by mismanagement, others by larger geopolitical or economic events. From the 1880s to 1910 the tequila industry prospered. Around 1910, however, the growth of tequila was curtailed during the Mexican Revolution but bounced back in the 1920s because of demand generated during Prohibition in the USA. The economic crisis caused by the Great Depression closed all but eight distilleries, and land reform reduced agave cultivation by two-thirds. After World War II, demand in the USA pushed sales higher but, when the industry doubled production in a five-year period, supply stagnated due to overharvesting of agave. Between 1968 and 1973, sales then boomed again, in part because of the 1968 Mexico City Olympics and the popularity of the Tequila Sunrise cocktail. In the 1990s, demand grew again, but underplanting – combined with a disease that wiped out almost one-third of the total crop – led to the closure of 20 distilleries by the end of the decade. The resulting shortage of agave caused the prices for ripe

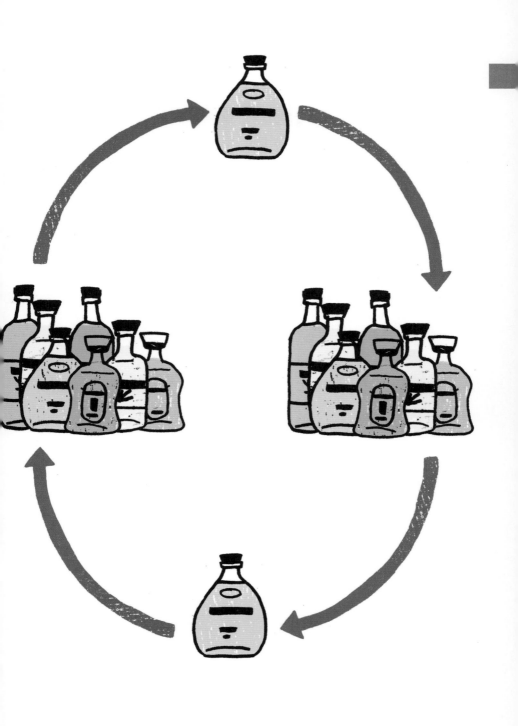

piñas to skyrocket, which in turn encouraged growers to plant more. This caused a glut in the market around 2007, which in turn sent prices plummeting. As a result, agave-growers stopped planting, and now we are once again facing a significant agave shortage even as demand for both 100 percent agave tequila and mezcal are growing by double digits.

Brick oven | PRODUCTION

One of several means available to producers of agave spirits (tequila, mezcal, etc.) for cooking piñas before fermentation. In tequila, brick ovens for cooking piñas were introduced around the middle of the 19th century. Unlike cooking the piñas in hornos (earthen pit ovens), which can give the spirit a smoky flavour, brick ovens were above ground and used indirect steam heat to cook the piñas, allowing more of the agave flavour to come through. The use of brick ovens was an important development in the history of tequila, and, according to US author Ian Chadwick, this is what made tequila a unique spirit and not just another style of mezcal produced in Jalisco. Today, the use of brick ovens is seen by many enthusiasts as one marker of a traditional tequila. Brick ovens are not as efficient as autoclaves, and it can take up to 72 hours for the piñas to fully cook.

Brix

See "Piña" (page 190).

Brown-Forman | BRAND

Founded in 1870 by George Garvin Brown, in Louisville, Kentucky, Brown began his business reselling bourbon and other bulk whiskeys. For the first 95 years, Brown-Forman was focused on the production of American whiskey. However, in 1966, the company purchased both Old Bushmills Irish Whiskey and Pepe Lopez, a mixto tequila brand. Then, in 2007, Brown-Forman purchased both Don Eduardo Tequila and Casa Herradura, which included El Jimador Tequila. With these purchases, Brown-Forman is now one of the largest producers of tequila in the world.

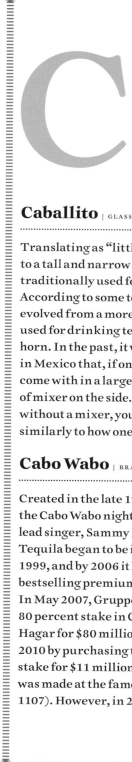

Caballito | GLASSWARE

Translating as "little horse", caballito refers
to a tall and narrow shot glass that has been
traditionally used for drinking tequila.
According to some tequila producers, the glass
evolved from a more traditional drinking vessel
used for drinking tequila, a hollowed-out bull's
horn. In the past, it was commonly understood
in Mexico that, if one ordered a tequila, it would
come with in a large glass of cola or another sort
of mixer on the side. If you wanted just the tequila
without a mixer, you would order a caballito,
similarly to how one would use the term "neat".

Cabo Wabo | BRAND

Created in the late 1990s as a house tequila for
the Cabo Wabo nightclub owned by Van Halen
lead singer, Sammy Hagar. Hagar's Cabo Wabo
Tequila began to be imported into the USA in
1999, and by 2006 it had grown to be the second
bestselling premium tequila in the country.
In May 2007, Gruppo Campari purchased an
80 percent stake in Cabo Wabo Tequila from
Hagar for $80 million, and followed it up in
2010 by purchasing the remaining 20 percent
stake for $11 million. At one point, Cabo Wabo
was made at the famed Tequila el Viejito (NOM
1107). However, in 2009, production moved to

Destiladora San Nicolas (NOM 1440). Cabo Wabo is made similarly to Espolón, with the blanco bottled unaged, the reposado aged in American oak barrels from four to six months, and the añejo aged in American oak barrels for fourteen months.

SEE ALSO
Agavoni *p20*
Gruppo Campari *p118*
Mezcal Negroni *p159*

Campari | BRAND

A herbal aperitif, Campari was invented by Gaspare Campari in the Piedmont region of Italy in 1860. In 1904, Campari set up his first factory to produce the aperitif, which is roughly speaking a mix of equal parts alcohol, sugar syrup and distilled water, infused with oranges, rhubarb, ginseng and several other herbs. Depending on the country the liqueur is destined for, the final strength can vary between 20.5% and 28.5% ABV. Traditionally, Campari got its red colour from cochineal, an insect found mostly in South America, though some countries have switched from using this colourant (known as E120) to other types of red food colouring. The success of the drink has relied on its incredible versatility. While Italians drink Campari either straight or with soda water, it is a fantastic cocktail ingredient, adding both sweetness and bitter elements to the drink. With agave spirits, Campari can be found in both the Agavoni and the Mezcal Negroni, both variations of the classic 1919 cocktail, the Negroni.

SEE ALSO
Agave *p16*
Jimador *p137*
Piña *p190*

Campesino | PRODUCTION

In the tequila business, campesinos – Spanish for "farmers" or "labourers" – do the work of planting, weeding, spraying pesticides and taking care of any other field labour, save for selecting and harvesting the piñas. From the

1800s to about the 1930s, agave cultivation took place on large estates, some of which were controlled by the major distilleries. Then, as today, the campesinos were responsible for all the labour but worked either as tenant farmers or day labourers. In the 1930s, Mexico went through a period of land redistribution and the campesinos were given a stake in the land they worked. Unfortunately, numerous cycles of boom and bust have reversed these efforts with the land for cultivation returning to a smaller and smaller number of owners, who hire day labourers who are not entitled to any benefits or job security.

Caramel colouring | ADDITIVE

A tequila additive that may be used to colour gold, reposado, añejo and extra añejo tequilas. Caramel colouring is a water-soluble food colouring that is derived from heating carbohydrates such as refined sugar, fructose, dextrose and so on. Caramel colouring used in distilled spirits such as tequila is also known as plain caramel, spirit caramel or E150a. Unlike caramel candy, caramel colouring is more fully oxidized and in its concentrated form appears black. However, when added to spirits in small quantities, the colour can range from pale yellow to a dark brown. Most gold tequilas are unaged mixto tequilas that have had caramel colouring added. And, even though reposado, añejo and extra añejo tequilas pick up some colour from resting in a barrel, the producer is allowed to add caramel colouring, either to standardize the colour batch to batch or to match consumer expectations for aged spirits.

Casa Noble | BRAND

Co-founded by Jose "Pepe" Hermosillo in 1996, Casa Noble is a contemporary expression of his family's 200-plus years experience growing and distilling blue agave. Casa Noble is made at La Cofradia (NOM 1137) and begins with organic blue agaves that are cooked for 36 hours in brick ovens, then milled, pressed for their juice and allowed to naturally ferment over five days. Once the must is fully fermented, it is distilled three times in stainless-steel stills with copper coils. Their core line consists of four tequilas, three of which are bottled at 40% ABV. Its blanco is unaged, its joven is matured between six and eight weeks in French oak and bottled at 51% ABV, its reposado is matured in used añejo barrels for 364 days (the legal maximum) and its añejo is matured for two years in new toasted French oak barrels. In 2014, Constellation Brands purchased Casa Noble.

Casamigos | BRAND

Created in 2013 by George Clooney, Rande Gerber and Mike Meldman, Casamigos was originally created as a house tequila for Clooney and Gerber, who had neighbouring properties in Cabo San Lucas, Mexico. After ordering 2,000 bottles over two years, the distillery Productos Finos de Agave (NOM 1416) asked the men to get a proper licence and purchase the tequila as a contract brand. At this point, Clooney, Gerber and Meldman decided to market the tequila in the USA. Taking on board the brand's growth and the people involved, Diageo purchased Casamigos from the partners in 2017 for $700 million, with an extra $300 million based on brand performance over the next ten years. The piñas are cooked in brick ovens, then pressed with a roller mill, fermented with and without the fibres, double distilled in copper pot stills, and bottled at 40% ABV. The blanco is rested for two months in stainless-steel vats to mellow, while the reposado and añejo are aged for seven and fourteen months, respectively, in used American whiskey barrels.

Cazadores | BRAND

The Cazadores distillery (NOM 1487) was founded in 1973 by Felix Bañuelos. Bañuelos had made his fortune in the dairy business and decided to make a tequila inspired by a story his grandfather told of seeing a large buck standing in a field of agave. The piñas are cooked for eight hours in large autoclaves and then placed in a diffuser that shreds and strips every gram of sugar from the piñas before the juice is sent to the fermenters. The must ferments for four days without the agave fibres. Once the primary fermentation is finished, Cazadores uses a process known as malolactic fermentation, a method usually employed by winemakers. From there the fermented must is double distilled in large stainless-steel pot stills and all of the tequilas are bottled at 40% ABV. The blanco is unaged, the reposado is aged just under one year, while the añejo is aged just over one year. Lastly, the extra añejo is aged for a minimum of three years in oak barrels. In 2002, Cazadores Tequila and its distillery were purchased by Bacardi Ltd for an undisclosed sum.

Centzon Totochtin | HISTORY

The Aztec gods of drunkenness, the Centzon Totochtin were a group of divine party-going

SEE ALSO
Bacardi Ltd *p35*
Column still *p67*
Diffuser *p87*
Must *p164*
Normas Oficiales Mexicanas
(NOM) *p171*
Patrón *p184*

SEE ALSO
Mayahuel *p152*
Pulque *p196*

rabbits who drank pulque in excess. The Centzon Totochtin – meaning "400 rabbits" – were said to be the children of Mayahuel, the goddess of fertility and the maguey (agave), who nursed her children with the fermented sap of the agave plant. The Centzon Totochtin represented the near-infinite number of mental states a human can possess while intoxicated. Some represented more positive aspects of drunkenness such as mirth, dancing, an increased sex drive and the origins of culture, while others represented darker characteristics such as hangovers, impaired vision and even suicide. Today, the Centzon Totochtin are still associated with pulque and agave spirits, with several brands using rabbits in their artwork and branding.

Chihuahua | REGION

SEE ALSO
Denomination of Origin for
  Sotol (DOS) *p80*
Norma Bebidas Alcohólicas
  Sotol *p168*
Sotol *p217*

Located in north-west Mexico, Chihuahua is the largest state in the country, just slightly bigger than the United Kingdom or only a little smaller than the USA state of Michigan. While Chihuahua is known for its large desert, the state also has large areas of grassland as well as humid and subtropical forests. Ciudad Juárez, which borders El Paso, Texas, is the largest city in the state and is home to many industrial and manufacturing companies, though it struggles with high levels of cartel violence. In addition to manufacturing, Chihuahua is the largest producer of oats, cotton, apples and pecan among other things, including sotol. Sotol is a distilled spirit made from the eponymous plant that grows in the rocky and arid deserts of eastern Chihuahua.

Chinaco | BRAND

Chinaco Tequila was created in 1977 at Tequilera La Gonzaleña (NOM 1127), the first legal tequila distillery built in the state of Tamaulípas. All the Chinaco tequilas start with piñas cooked in an autoclave, which are then crushed with a roller mill. The must is fermented and double distilled in stainless-steel pot stills with copper coils. After distillation, the spirit is allowed to rest for a short time, and a portion is used to bottle the blanco unaged at 40% ABV. The reposado matures between eight and eleven months in French and English oak barrels, while the añejo is a blend of tequilas aged for 30 months in French and English oak with another portion matured in used bourbon barrels made from American oak casks.

Clone | PLANT

A biological organism that is created asexually and is genetically identical to its source organism. In the tequila world, most agave plants are reproduced through cloning. Most agaves have two forms of reproduction, self-cloning by creating offshoots called hijuelos or by seeds that are pollinated, usually by bats. However, agave plants can also be cloned by taking cuttings of the plant. Once a young agave has multiple leaves growing from its base, one of the full leaves (pencas) can be removed and new roots will begin to grow from the penca, which can then be replanted. Reproducing agaves through cloning is fast and efficient. Over time, however, repeated cloning can make the plants susceptible to new pests and diseases. If most of an agave plantation is growing a small number of clones, then the plantation is susceptible to complete

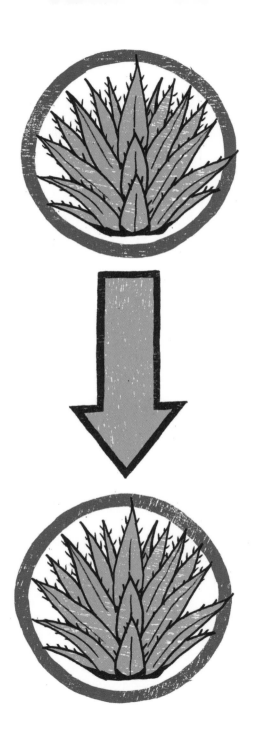

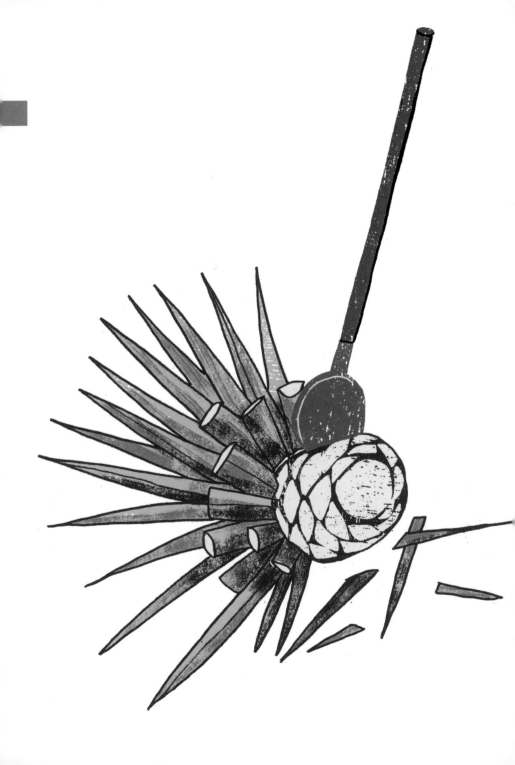

crop failure or a population crash if the "right" pest gains a foothold.

Coa de jima | PRODUCTION

SEE ALSO
Agave *p16*
Jimador *p137*
Piña *p190*

A long-handled hoe with a rounded blade on the end, used to harvest agave. The coa de jima is wielded by a jimador who uses it to first remove the pencas (leaves of the agave), which are often large and spiked with thorns. Because of the shape of the coa and its long handle, after some of the outer leaves are removed, the jimador is able to detach the agave from the roots and then begin to shave the leaves off until the piña is exposed. Once the leaves are removed, the pattern exposed resembles a pineapple, which is why the agave heads are referred to as piñas. After the jimador has finished their job, the piñas are carried to a truck and carted off to the distillery.

Cointreau | BRAND

SEE ALSO
Curaçao *p74*
Margarita *p149*
Picador *p189*
Tequila Daisy *p227*
Triple sec *p237*

First sold in 1875 by brothers Edouard-Jean and Adolphe Cointreau, Cointreau as it is known today was first called Curaçao Blanco Triple Sec. The Cointreau curaçao was unique because it used both sweet and bitter orange peels distilled three times in a neutral base spirit made from beetroot sugars. In 1923, the Curaçao Blanco Triple Sec, now simply known as Cointreau, entered the American market and became a very popular cocktail ingredient. Used in more than 350 cocktails, Cointreau is an excellent orange-flavoured liqueur that pairs very well with tequila and can be found in the Margarita, the Picador and the Tequila Daisy. In 1990, Rémy Martin and Cointreau merged to form Rémy Cointreau, the new owner and producer of the Cointreau orange-flavoured liqueur.

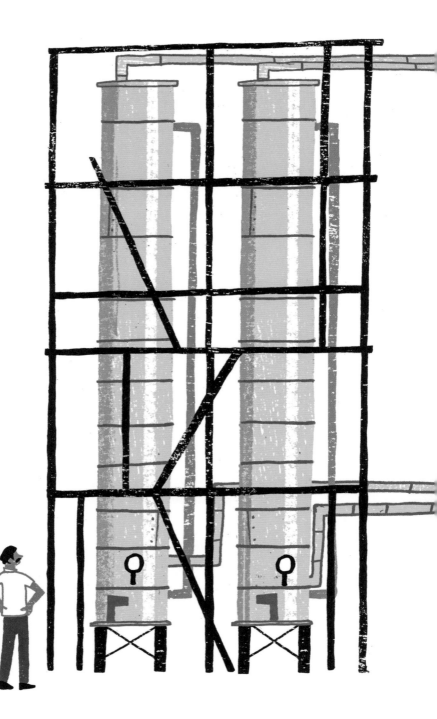

SEE ALSO
Proofing*p193*

Cold mixing | PRODUCTION

Also known as blending, cold mixing is the process of combining two or more distilled spirits, usually before proofing and bottling. According to Mexican regulations, tequila cannot be mixed with any spirit other than tequila. So blanco tequilas can be mixed together, or an añejo can be mixed with a reposado, and so on. When making a mixto tequila with less than 100 percent agave, one cannot combine 100 percent agave tequila with some other non-blue agave spirit. Instead, one must ferment the agave and non-agave sugars together and then distil it.

SEE ALSO
Alambique*p22*
Mixto *p163*

Column still | PRODUCTION

In 1830, Aeneas Coffey, an Irish excise tax collector, was granted a patent for two column stills in series that could be operated continuously, becoming one of the last major advancements in distilling technology. The Coffey still was the forerunner of the modern column still. It was highly efficient, could be fed non-stop and could produce spirits that were much cleaner than those made in other stills of its time. Coffey's design ideas for the continuous column still became so popular they are still in use today. In tequila production, the column still was a natural adaptation, and many of the largest mixto tequila brands and a few 100 percent agave tequilas are made using column stills. Because of the column still's efficiency, the resulting spirits are much more cost effective to produce. It also allows the distiller to create a cleaner and lighter spirit, which works especially well if it is intended for a mixto that will have caramel colouring and/or oak extracts added after distillation.

Condenser | PRODUCTION

The part of the still that condenses the spirit vapour back into a liquid before it is collected. On modern stills, the condenser can be a highly technical heat exchanger that runs chilled propylene glycol through a series of tubes or plates that surround the worm tube, the small-diameter tubing that channels the spirit vapour through the condenser and out to a collection tank. In modern distilleries, propylene glycol is used in the condenser because it has a lower freezing point than water and allows the spirit to phase change more quickly. In more traditional settings, it is not uncommon to see condensers that are little more than a large barrel of cold water with a coil or tubing on the inside of the barrel. Some distillers use the even more old-fashioned technique of placing a copper bowl on top of the still with cold water running onto the top, while on the underside the vapours condense and drip out the lyne arm.

Consejo Regulador del Mezcal (Mezcal Regulatory Council) | LAWS

Founded in 1997, the Consejo Mexicano Regulador de la Calidad del Mezcal (Council of Mexican Regulators for the Quality of Mezcal; COMERCAM) was established to act as the primary body responsible for certifying that producers of mezcal were following the provisions of NOM-070-SCFI. Around 2014, COMERCAM changed its name to the Consejo Regulador del Mezcal (CRM), and has presided over the mezcal industry's tremendous growth. Since 2012, the number of companies involved in the mezcal business has grown from 300 to about 1,200, and production increased from

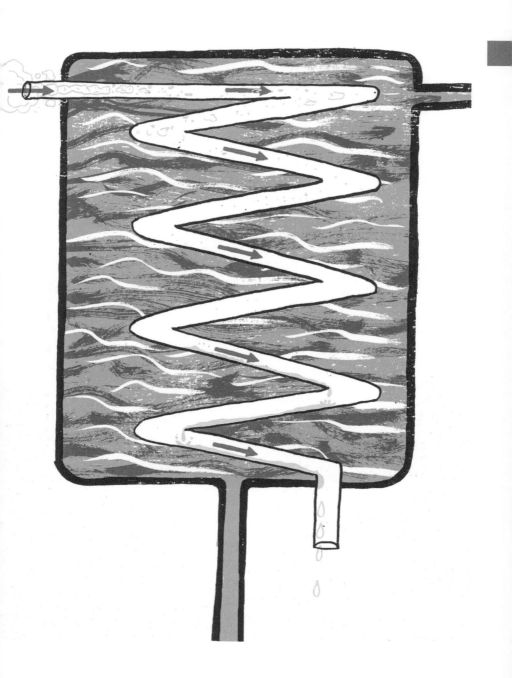

200,000 litres (about 52,800gal [US]) per year to 2 million litres (some 528,000gal [US]) per year, which has significantly increased the number of certifications that need processing as well as the vigilance required to defeat regulation-shy opportunists. The CRM is also responsible for taking action against fake and adulterated mezcal that can tarnish the reputation of this wonderful and fast-growing category.

Consejo Regulador del Tequila (Tequila Regulatory Council) | LAWS

SEE ALSO
Denomination of Origin for Tequila (DOT) p83
Normas Oficiales Mexicanas (NOM) p171

Founded in Guadalajara, Jalisco, Mexico, in 1994, the Consejo Regulador del Tequila (CRT) is a private non-profit organization made up of agave growers, tequila producers, tequila bottlers, marketers and members of the Mexican government. The CRT is tasked with ensuring that producers, bottlers and marketers are compliant with the Normas Oficiales Mexicanas (NOM) for Tequila through inspections and certification; guaranteeing the purity of commercial tequila; protecting the Denomination of Origin for Tequila (DOT) in Mexico and internationally, and providing information about tequila. Recently, the CRT has exercised its protection powers by threatening to sue a major brand of beer for making a tequila-flavoured beer that did not actually have any tequila in it, while also helping to seize almost 200,000 litres (about 52,800gal [US]) of fake tequila intended for the open market.

Craft tequila | CLASSIFICATION

A catchy term that is not regulated by the Mexican government. Many people tend to think of craft spirits as some combination of

small production, traditional techniques and/ or independent ownership of the distillery that produced the spirit. Mike Morales of Tequila Aficionado argues that the USA definitions for craft beer and spirits should not be applied to tequila and instead offers his craft tequila gauntlet that can help select, define and measure a craft tequila. The gauntlet considers seven markers, including, among others, the pedigree of the owners, the ownership of the distillery, production processes and transparency. Using it, one should be able to determine the craft credentials of any particular tequila brand.

Cristalino | CLASSIFICATION

An unregulated term that refers to barrel-aged tequilas (reposados, añejos or extra añejos) that have had the colour stripped out of them to make the spirit crystal-clear, similar to a blanco tequila. This has been a common practice in the rum world, and recently tequila producers have begun to use this practice as well. The advantage of creating a cristalino tequila is that the spirit retains the flavour and the oxidative effects that tend to soften spirits that have been matured in a barrel but without the associated colour. Some people prefer clear spirits for aesthetic reasons, and you will find that some bartenders like to use decolourized spirits for the purpose of preserving the colour of the cocktail they are making. In order to achieve this clear effect, the matured spirit is filtered using a pulverized or powdered activated carbon that has a lot of surface area and a large number of macropores. This allows the activated carbon to quickly absorb the colour compounds, leaving the matured spirit crystal-clear but with virtually the same aroma and flavour.

SEE ALSO
Grand Marnier *p117*
Triple sec *p237*

Curaçao | COCKTAIL INGREDIENT

A liqueur flavoured with laraha citrus named after the island of Curaçao located in the southern Caribbean Sea, north of Venezuela. The flavours of tequila pair very well with citrus, and many tequila cocktails call for orange liqueur to add both sweetness and flavour. Curaçao can be used in many of these cocktails instead of triple sec or some other orange-flavoured liqueur. In 1527, Spanish explorers brought the Seville orange (*Citrus aurantium*) to the island. However, this variety did not adapt well to the climate, and after some time a new subspecies of bitter, fibrous oranges with aromatic green skins (*C. aurantium* var. *currassuviencis*) developed on the island. Dried laraha skins eventually became a commodity and were used as a flavouring agent. By the late 1800s, laraha began showing up as the primary flavouring agent of the liqueur that became known as curaçao.

Deforestation | ENVIRONMENT

The process by which forests or stands of trees
are removed to repurpose the land for other
commercial uses or for resource extraction
without sufficient replanting of trees. When
an area is deforested, it can cause a drop in the
biodiversity of the environment, give a foothold
to invasive species of plants or animals and
increase aridity and soil erosion. Today, parts
of Mexico are facing significant deforestation
due to increased demand for firewood without
sufficient replanting to offset the extraction. The
current Normas Oficiales Mexicanas (NOM)
for mezcal production created two value-added
categories to reflect and protect traditional
distilling practices. Both mezcal ancestral
and mezcal artesanal require the use of fire at
different points in the production process and,
owing to limited infrastructure, most of that
fire is generated through the burning of wood.
As mezcal production has grown, the demand
for firewood, particularly in Oaxaca, has grown
significantly. This demand has contributed
to the deforestation of parts of Mexico and the
importation of firewood from outside Oaxaca.

SEE ALSO
Denomination of Origin for
Mezcal (DOM) *p80*
Madurado en vidrio *p149*

Demijohn | PRODUCTION

Also known as a carboy, a demijohn is a large glass vessel with a narrow neck. The demijohn has been used as a container for fermenting beer, wine and cider as well as for storing distilled spirits. In France, it is common for brandy producers to store aged spirits in demijohns after they have reached the ideal maturity. According to the regulations for mezcal (NOM-070-SCFI), once the final spirit run is finished, mezcal not going into a barrel for maturing is stored in glass or stainless-steel containers. If the producer chooses, they may store mezcal in demijohns for a minimum of 12 months and label them as madurado en vidrio. Because glass is air permeable, the spirit can breathe and oxidize, giving it the benefits of maturation without the addition of flavours from the wood barrel.

SEE ALSO
Normas Oficiales Mexicanas
(NOM) *p171*

Denomination of Origin (DO) | LAWS

A declaration that only a product (usually a food stuff) made within a nominated state or country may use a particular name, because it is a unique product defined by its materials, production and geography – for example, tequila. Sometimes referred to as an appellation, denominations of origin have no legal authority outside the country in which they are issued, although countries that enter into trade agreements usually also include reciprocal protections for items that have an established Denomination of Origin (DO). The first recognized DO in the West was created in 1716 when Cosimo III de' Medici, Grand Duke of Tuscany, ruled that only wine produced in the villages of Castellina, Gaiole, Radda, Greve and another small area could use the name Chianti. After this, other European

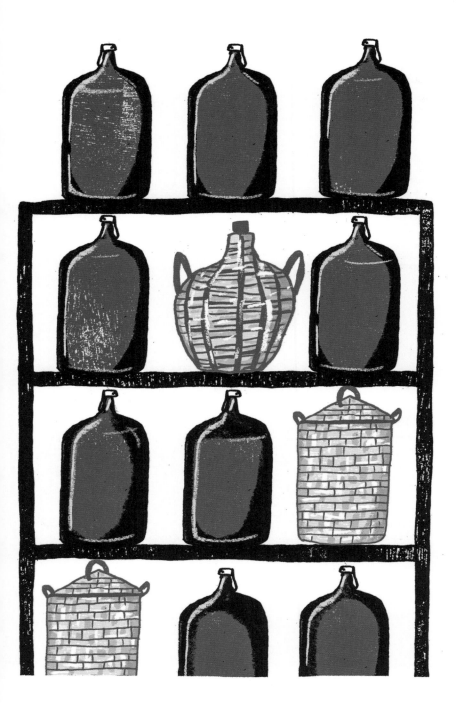

countries began to follow suit, creating systems to identify and protect national products of significant historical value. In 1974, Mexico created its first Denomination of Origin (DO) for the alcoholic beverage known as tequila.

SEE ALSO
Bacanora *p35*
Espadin *p103*
Sonora *p214*

Denomination of Origin for Bacanora (DOB) | LAWS

Originally established in 2000, the NOM-168-SCFI defining the rules for bacanora was last updated in 2004. Bacanora is defined as the distilled spirits of *Agave angustifolia* Haw., also known as espadin in Oaxaca, and produced in 35 municipalities surrounding the town of Bacanora in the Mexican state of Sonora. Producers may use wild and/or cultivated *A. angustifolia* grown in the denomination zone to make bacanora. The piñas must be cooked (to hydrolyse the agave sugars) and milled before the must is fermented with yeast. Post-distillation, the alcoholic strength of bacanora may be adjusted only with the addition of demineralized or distilled water and bottled between 38% and 55% ABV. Similar to tequila and mezcal, bacanora can come in four categories: blanco/silver, which is unaged; joven/gold, which is a blend of aged and unaged bacanora; reposado/aged, which must spend a minimum of two months in oak barrels no larger than 200 litres (about 53gal [US]); and añejo/extra aged, which must be matured for a minimum of one year. Interestingly, any age statements labelled for reposado or añejo bacanoras may be given as the weighted average of the ages and volumes of the components in the bottle.

Denomination of Origin for Mezcal (DOM) | LAWS

While mezcal has been made in Mexico for hundreds of years, the spirit did not receive a Denomination of Origin (DO) until 1994, when the National Chamber of the Mezcal Industry petitioned for its recognition. Originally, the DO covered just Durango, San Luis Potosí, Guerrero, Zacatecas and Oaxaca. However, over time, the DO region has been expanded to include select municipalities in Tamaulipas, Guanajuato, Puebla and Michoacán. When the DO for mezcal was written, it modelled itself after the DO for tequila. Initially, the DO for mezcal contained two categories: 100 percent agave mezcals and mezcals that are allowed to contain up to 40 percent of their fermentable sugars from other sources. However, this mixto mezcal has since been removed from the regulation (NOM-070-SCFI) that governs its production. The original DO also stipulated that mezcal should be colourless unless it is aged, in which case reposado and añejo mezcals are allowed to have a yellowish colour.

Denomination of Origin for Sotol (DOS) | LAWS

In January 2001, the Ministry of the Economy for the Mexican state of Chihuahua campaigned to have the government issue a Denomination of Origin (DO) for sotol. After a period of public comment, the DO for sotol was passed in August 2002, and the Normas Oficiales Mexicanas (NOM) that regulate its production were issued in June 2004. The DO declared that sotol is a distilled spirit obtained from either wild or cultivated dasylirion plants commonly known

as sotol or sereque, in the states of Chihuahua, Coahuila and Durango. Interestingly, the DO for sotol recounts the history of the drink in the region. Before the colonial period, dasylirion (*Dasylirion* spp.) was used for food and making baskets, but in the 16th century the Franciscans brought distillation technology to the region, and sotol became not just a food but a distilled beverage. The DO also describes the dasylirion habitat, which sits in the Mexican Central Plateau at 1,000–2,000m (3,280–6,560ft) above sea level between the Sierra Madre Oriental and the Sierra Madre Occidental mountains.

Denomination of Origin for Tequila (DOT) | LAWS

As with all agave spirits in Mexico, tequila has about 400 years of history and tradition in and around the municipal town of Tequila. Initially, tequila was just a mezcal made like any other agave spirit in Mexico, but around the end of the 19th century distillers began to transition their process for cooking the agave from hornos (earthen pit ovens) to brick ovens that cook with indirect heat. At the same time, this is when distillers began to refer to their spirits as mezcal de tequila and then just tequila. In the 1940s, Mexico began to pass a series of laws to regulate tequila production, although the first Normas Oficiales Mexicanas (NOM) for tequila were not passed until 1964. After World War II, tequila's popularity continued to grow, and it received worldwide attention during the 1968 Mexico City Olympics. It was at this time that tequila producers began to see knock-off "tequila" spirits being made in Asia and Europe, so the Regional Chamber of the Tequila Industry applied for a Denomination of Origin (DO) to help protect tequila internationally. The DO was granted in December 1974, and it received recognition from the World Industrial Property Organization in 1978.

Desquiote | PLANT

SEE ALSO
Bats *p39*
Quiote *p199*

The process by which the quiote is removed from a maturing agave plant. Also referred to as castration, removing the quiote causes the agave to put its energy into developing its store of inulin, thereby increasing the potential alcohol from the plant, instead of channelling its energy into growing the quiote and sexual reproduction. Agave spirits that receive the "Bat Friendly" certification verify that they allow 5 percent of their agave plants to flower while the remaining 95 percent are castrated to produce agaves with more reserves of carbohydrates that can be fermented into alcohol.

Diageo | BRAND

SEE ALSO
Casamigos *p57*
Don Julio *p92*

The world's largest producer of distilled spirits, Diageo was created in 1997 from the merger of Guinness and Grand Metropolitan. Diageo owns some of the largest spirit brands in the world, including Johnnie Walker Blended Scotch Whisky and Smirnoff Vodka. Diageo entered the tequila market in 2003 with the purchase of a 50 percent stake in Don Julio Tequila. In 2012, Diageo entered talks to purchase all of Jose Cuervo Tequila but after 18 months no deal was reached. When talks with Cuervo fell through, Diageo purchased Peligroso Tequila and a 50 percent stake in DeLeón Tequila owned by Sean Combs in 2014, followed in 2015 with the total acquisition of Don Julio from Cuervo in exchange for Bushmills Irish Whiskey and

$408 million in cash. Continuing their tequila buying spree, Diageo purchased Casamigos, a brand started by George Clooney, Rande Gerber and Mike Meldman for $1 billion. Shortly after purchasing Casamigos, Diageo announced that the brand would add an artisanal mezcal to the Casamigos lineup. And, in May 2018, Diageo announced that they were purchasing Pierde Almas Mezcal for an undisclosed sum.

Diffuser | PRODUCTION

A modern piece of equipment that is designed to remove agave sugars from the piñas without cooking. A diffuser looks like a very large conveyor belt that intakes agave piñas and processes them, so the sugars can be fermented and distilled. In most instances, whole, raw piñas are loaded into a hopper that carries the piñas on a conveyor belt into the machine. Once in the machine, the piñas are shredded and the pulp is washed in a solution that dissolves the agave inulin. Inulin is a soluble fibre that, when heated, breaks down into fructose, sucrose and glucose. Once the inulin is liquefied, it is separated from the pulp and pumped into large autoclaves (the pulp can be dried and used for a variety of purposes). The diffuser is about 99 percent efficient in extracting potential fermentable sugars compared to the 70 percent when a brick oven and tahona are used. However, there is a change (not considered for the better) in the flavour profile of tequilas made with a diffuser compared to other, less efficient means.

Distillation | PRODUCTION

The process by which different chemical compounds are separated and concentrated based on their relative boiling points. As a liquid such as beer or wine is heated, volatile compounds such as acetone and methanol begin to evaporate first because they have a lower boiling point than water. As the contents continue to heat up, ethanol will start to volatilize and separate from the rest of the liquid. Distillation captures these vapours and recondenses them into liquid, with the various parts saved for their intended uses, such as beverage alcohol. Humans have been practising distillation for thousands of years with some of the earliest evidence found in *The Epic of Gilgamesh* (*c.* 2150 BCE). There is an ongoing academic discussion of when distilling came to Mesoamerica. While there is evidence that Asian sailors brought still technology (olla de barro) to western Mexico, it is not conclusive if this happened before or at the same time as contact with Europeans.

SEE ALSO
Mezcal *p155*
Sotol *p217*
Tequila *p222*

Distiller | PRODUCTION

A person who runs a still or supervises the production of spirits. In Mexico, distillers are referred to by the type of spirit they make. A distiller who makes tequila is referred to as a tequilero; a distiller who makes mezcal is called a mezcalero; a distiller who makes sotol is a sotolero and so on. Depending on the size of the distillery, some distillers are also the owner and handle all of the production, while in larger distilleries the distiller supervises production and acts as a manager and performs quality control. The terms "master mezcalero", "master tequilero" and so on are not legally defined, but in practice these terms are best reserved for those who have decades of experience making the spirits.

Distillery | PRODUCTION

The site where distillation takes place. In Mexico, distilleries go by a few different names, depending on the region of the country. Distillery simply translates as *destilería*. However, it is common in Jalisco for tequila distilleries to be referred to as *fábricas* (factories), while in Oaxaca and much of the mezcal world distilleries are referred to as *palenques*. These different names do not seem to have any legal or technical differences but rather represent a difference in tradition and local culture.

Don Cenobio Sauza | PEOPLE

Don Cenobio Sauza got his start in the tequila business working for Jose Cuervo but, in 1873, he purchased a distillery, which he called La Preservancia. Among the vanguard of the tequila business, Sauza switched from using a horno (earthen pit oven) to cook his agaves to aboveground brick ovens that used indirect heat and cooked the agaves without imparting a smoky flavour. Sauza also was one of the first tequileros to begin exporting his tequila to the USA, which eventually became the largest market for tequila in the world. Between 1873 and his death in 1906, Sauza amassed an empire, purchasing 13 distilleries and about 300 agave plantations, becoming the second largest tequila producer after Jose Cuervo. After his death, his son Eladio Sauza took control of the company and continued his father's legacy.

Don Jose Antonio de Cuervo | PEOPLE

Patriarch of the Cuervo family empire, Jose Antonio de Cuervo became a distiller when, in

1758, he inherited his family's hacienda, which consisted of agave fields and a small distillery. Cuervo managed the hacienda and grew the distillery and increased production to about 800,000 litres (about 211,300gal [US]) of mezcal a year. Cuervo's success was short lived when King Charles III banned all Mexican production of alcoholic beverages in an attempt to promote the consumption of Spanish brandy, wine and sherry. Ten years later Cuervo had passed away, and his son Jose Maria Guadalupe Cuervo restarted the distillery when King Charles IV lifted the ban on Mexican alcohol and Jose Maria received an official licence from the crown to produce and sell mezcal.

SEE ALSO
Diageo *p84*
Don Julio González-Frausto
Estrada *p94*

Don Julio | BRAND

Created in 1987, Don Julio Tequila, now owned by Diageo, is one of first and bestselling premium tequilas in terms of value. In 2017, Don Julio sold 1.3 million 9-litre (2.38gal [US]) cases worldwide. The tequila was originally intended solely to serve to guests at Don Julio González-Frausto Estrada's 60th birthday party, but it was deemed special enough that Don Julio decided to launch a new brand with it. The agaves are cooked in brick ovens, milled, fermented and double distilled in stainless-steel stills with copper coils. The blanco tequila is unaged and bottled between 38% and 40% ABV depending on the country of sale. The reposado is aged for eight months in American white-oak barrels while the añejo is aged for a minimum of eighteen months. The brand's Don Julio 70 takes the same 18-month añejo tequila but strips out the colour with activated charcoal. The Don Julio 1942 commemorates the year of the company's founding and is aged for a minimum of two and a

half years in American white oak. Lastly, the Don Julio Real is an extra-añejo tequila that is a blend of tequilas aged between three and five years.

Don Julio González-Frausto Estrada | PEOPLE

Don Julio González-Frausto Estrada (González) was born in 1925 and began working at an early age in his uncle's tequila distillery. When González was 15, his father passed away, so he began selling barrels of tequila to help support his family. At the age of 17, he got a loan and purchased the La Primavera, an agave estate with an attached distillery, now called the Tequila Don Julio Distillery (NOM 1449). For 40 years, González honed his craft and the Tres Magueyes tequila brand until the creation of his eponymous brand. González decided to put Don Julio Tequila in a squat bottle so that it could remain on the table without it getting in the way of people's conversations. In 1999, González sold his company to Seagram, which happened to go bankrupt a year later. The Don Julio brand passed from Jose Cuervo in 2000 to Diageo in 2014, two years after González passed away.

Double distilled | PRODUCTION

The process by which a spirit is distilled twice to concentrate desirable flavours and aromas while removing non-desirable flavours and toxic compounds. A fermented liquid that goes into a still between 4% and 12% ABV will come out after the first distillation run somewhere between 30% and 55% ABV; this is often referred to as a "low wine". Because the low wines often come out below 40% ABV and there are still some unpleasant elements to the spirit, it has been

D

94

SEE ALSO
Don Julio *p92*
Normas Oficiales Mexicanas
(NOM) *p171*

SEE ALSO
Distillation *p87*

common practice when using a pot still to distil most spirits twice. The low wines will go into the still around 30% ABV, and after the second distillation run the end product comes out between 60% and 80% ABV. This spirit is purer and has a more concentrated aroma and flavour. If the spirit is intended to be consumed unaged, the producer will add water to bring down the alcohol concentration to bottling strength, usually around 40% ABV.

SEE ALSO
Denomination of Origin for
  Mezcal (DOM) *p80*
Denomination of Origin for
  Sotol (DOS) *p80*

Durango | REGION

Located in north-west Mexico, Durango has the second lowest population density of any state in the country. Durango has an average elevation of 2,000m (6,560ft) above sea level, and much of the state is dominated by the Sierra Madre Occidental mountains. Known as the "land of the scorpions", Durango has a rich food culture, featuring green and red chillies as well as locally made cheeses and preserves. In addition to these foods, Durango is included in the Denomination of Origin (DO) for both sotol and mezcal. Because these two spirits are made from different plants – dasylirion and agave, respectively – it is permitted for these DOs to overlap. In addition to espadin, mezcals made in Durango by small artisan distillers use *Agave cenizo* and *Agave durangensis*.

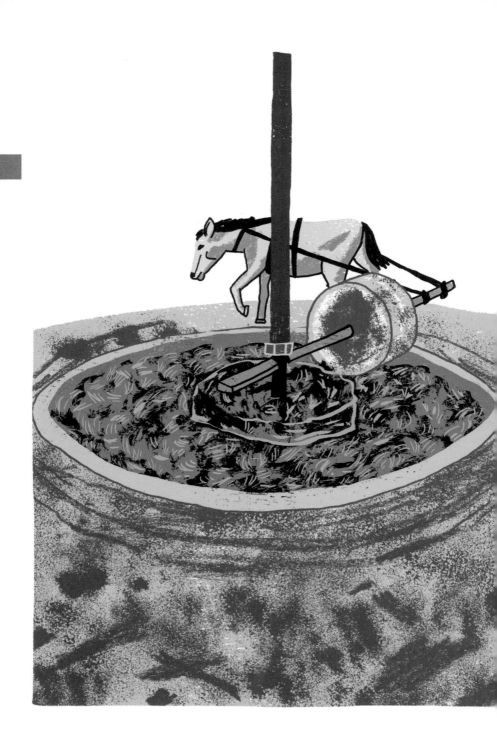

Egyptian mill | PRODUCTION

A shallow well, made of cement or stone, in which cooked agave is pressed and ground before moving to the fermenters. The Egyptian mill is also combined with a tahona, a large rock or cement wheel traditionally pulled in a circle by a mule, horse or ox. The tahona is attached to a central axis in the mill and, as the stone rolls, its heavy weight crushes and compresses the cooked piñas inside the well. Egyptian mills are still used for some traditionally made 100 percent agave tequilas as well as for ancestral and artisanal mezcals.

El Jimador | BRAND

Created in 1994 by Casa Herradura, El Jimador, now owned by Brown-Forman, is meant to honour the industrious workers who harvest agave by hand every day. In 2017, El Jimador sold 1.2 million 9-litre (2.38gal [US]) cases, making it one of the top-selling tequilas in the world. El Jimador is made using a diffuser and a stainless-steel column still. The unaged tequila is used for the silver expression tequila as well as the flavoured tequilas (lime, mango and cinnamon) and a line of ready-to-drink cocktails. El Jimador Reposado spends two months in American oak barrels, and the añejo also spends twelve months in American oak barrels, which most likely previously held Old Forester Bourbon or perhaps Jack Daniel's Tennessee Whiskey.

SEE ALSO
Normas Oficiales Mexicanas
(NOM) *p171*

El Viejito | BRAND

Founded in 1937 by Indalecio Núñez Muro in Los Altos de Jalisco, Tequila el Viejito (NOM 1107) is a family-run company known for producing excellent tequilas. The piñas are steamed in brick ovens for 16 hours, rest for 6 hours and then cook for another 14 hours. After cooking, the piñas are pressed using a roller mill and the juice is collected to ferment in 37,000-litre (9,774gal [US]) stainless-steel tanks. Once fermentation is done, the must is double distilled in copper pot stills. After distillation, some of the unaged tequila gets bottled either as Plata Cristalino at 42% ABV or Plata at 55% ABV. Their aged tequila goes into used bourbon barrels and are aged according to their type: reposado for two months, añejo for one year and extra añejo for three years.

SEE ALSO
Mezcal ancestral *p155*
Mezcal artesanal *p156*
Olla de barro *p177*

En barro | PRODUCTION

An unregulated term meaning "in clay" found on some bottles of mezcal to indicate that the spirit was made using a direct-fired clay still. Clay stills are allowed to be used for making ancestral and artisanal mezcal. It is common to see information such as agave type, fermentation vessel and still type listed on these bottles, so instead of the label saying "olla de barro", it may simply state "en barro".

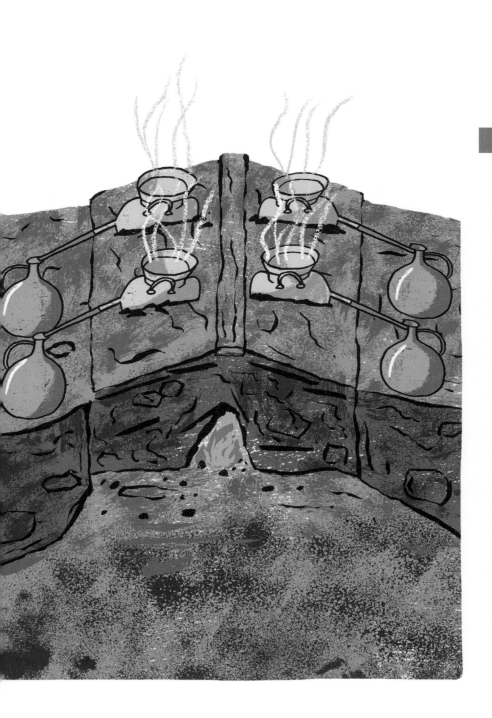

Enrique Fonseca | PEOPLE

A fourth-generation agave grower, Enrique Fonseca became a distiller by necessity when Cuervo and Sauza backed out of large contracts during an agave glut. The glut caused prices of agave to drop and Fonseca had to figure out what to do with his ripe agave or watch them rot in the field. Instead, he purchased La Tequileña (NOM 1146) from Bacardi, and with some help began distilling tequila using both pot and column stills, which he could then blend to control the final flavour and finish. At the same time, Fonseca began laying down barrels of tequila to age, but not just for a year or two but for a long time. Some of the oldest tequilas on the market are typically in the three- to four-year-old range but, in 2013, Fonseca began releasing some of the oldest tequilas from his stock of 20,000 ageing barrels, including a 21-year-old extra-añejo tequila – probably one of the oldest ever created.

Espadin (*Agave angustifolia*) | PLANT

The most common variety of agave used in mezcal production, *Agave angustifolia* has one of the largest growing ranges of any agave, extending from the American Southwest to southern Mexico. Most mezcaleros refer to the plant by its common name, espadin. Before European scientists created binomial nomenclature (two-term Latin names) for the different varieties of maguey, locals already had names for the plants that sometimes varied by region. For instance, in the Mexican state of Sonora, locals used a maguey called yaquiana to make the local spirit bacanora, while Oaxacans used a maguey called espadin to make mezcal. Recent scientific research has shown that both yaquiana and espadin are in fact both *A. angustifolia*.

Espolòn | BRAND

Created in 1998 by Cirilo Oropeza, Espolòn Tequila is named after the spur (Spanish: *espolòn*) on the back of a rooster's leg. Oropeza designed the Destiladora San Nicolas (NOM 1440) in Los Altos de Jalisco to make what he considered the perfect tequila. Espolòn is made by quartering and cooking the piñas for 22 hours in an autoclave, then the piñas are pressed using a roller mill and the wort (extracted liquid) is fermented for 72 hours in stainless-steel tanks. Espolòn distils some of its wort using a column still and some in a stainless-steel pot still. All the tequilas are a blend of the column-still and pot-still distillates, bottled at 40% ABV. The blanco is unaged, the reposado is matured for a minimum of three months in new American oak barrels, the añejo spends ten months in new American oak and then two more in used Wild Turkey bourbon barrels. In 2009, Gruppo Campari purchased Espalòn and Destiladora San Nicolas for $27.5 million.

Extra añejo | CLASSIFICATION

A regulated labelling term in Mexico as a non-specific age statement for tequila. Extra-añejo tequilas (mixto or 100 percent agave) must spend at least three years in an oak barrel or container that is no more than 600 litres (almost 160gal [US]) in volume. While one would assume that extra añejo would simply translate as "extra aged", that term is already used as the English translation for añejo tequilas. Therefore, if a producer wants to list an English translation

for extra añejo on their label, it must say "ultra aged". This labelling term was officially added to the regulations for tequila with the 2005 update for NOM-006-SCFI because a number of brands were maturing tequilas far in excess of one year. As an example, Herradura Seleccion Suprema, which was created in 1990, is aged for 49 months before it is bottled.

SEE ALSO
Normas Oficiales Mexicanas
(NOM) *p171*
Tapatio *p221*

Familia Camarena | BRAND

The Camarena family has been distilling tequila
since 1937, and, as the family has grown, new
members have taken up the family legacy.
When Mauricio Camarena created the Familia
Camarena tequila brand, it was originally
made at Tequila Tapatio (NOM 1139) by Carlos
Camarena. Today, however, Familia Camarena
tequilas are made at Casa Tequilera Herencia de
Los Altos (NOM 1569). The tequila is made from
piñas processed with a diffuser, fermented in
stainless-steel tanks, and distilled on a column
still. Familia Camarena tequilas come in two
expressions: an unaged silver tequila bottled at
40% ABV, and a reposado, which is matured in
oak barrels for two months before being bottled
at 40% ABV. In the USA, Familia Camarena
tequilas are imported and distributed by E. & J.
Gallo Winery based in California.

SEE ALSO
Mezcal *p155*
Must *p164*
Natural fermentation *p167*
Tequila *p222*

Fermentation | PRODUCTION

A chemical breakdown of food or other organic
material by microorganisms such as yeast
or bacteria. For alcoholic beverages, yeast
consumes simple sugars and produces alcohol,
heat, carbon dioxide and hundreds of other
esters that are aromatic and flavourful. In
Mexico, most agave spirits are allowed to use

both cultivated and wild yeasts. Cultivated yeasts are those strains that over the centuries have been known to have high alcohol tolerances and produce good flavours from their base material. Wild yeasts, often referred to in relation to natural fermentation, are uncultivated strains that float in the air and settle on plants and structures. Fermentations done with wild yeasts usually take longer to attenuate (fully convert all of the available sugars into alcohol) and can produce off flavours and aromas. Fermentation is a necessary step in making any distilled spirit, including tequila and mezcal. Depending on the amount of available sugar, nutrients and the type of yeast, an agave ferment can take between three days to two weeks and produce a must (mosto) of between 4% and 8% ABV.

French oak *(Quercus robur)* | PLANT

SEE ALSO
Holm oak *p129*
White oak *p241*

One of the most common European species of oak used for storing wine and spirits. Because of the cooler climate compared with the American Midwest, French oak tends to have a tighter grain than American white oak and is less dense. This means that, in general, wine and spirits enter the wood more slowly and so take on more subtle flavours in addition to notes of spice such as pepper. French oak is a good choice for barrels when the distiller wants to add dryness and spice but without a lot of oak or vanilla flavours common to American white oak.

Fuenteseca | BRAND

SEE ALSO
Enrique Fonseca *p103*
Extra añejo *p104*
Must *p164*
Normas Oficiales Mexicanas
  (NOM) *p171*

Created in 2013, as a collaboration between Enrique Fonseca (NOM 11460) and Jake Lustig of Haas Brothers in San Francisco to bottle some of the oldest and most elegant tequilas ever made.

Fonseca is a fourth-generation agave grower and distiller in Los Altos de Jalisco. Fonseca and Lustig created Fuenteseca to showcase what is possible when tequila is matured for four, seven, nine, eleven, even twenty-one years in used barrels that do not impart too much oak and overpower the spirit. First, the piñas are cooked in depressurized autoclaves. They are then shredded and pressed with a screw mill, before being fermented. The fermented must is distilled using a column still, stainless-steel pot and copper pot stills, and these individual distillates are then matured in used barrels from a variety of sources. When it is time to bottle, Fonseca can create perfect blends by mixing, for example, column-still tequila aged in wine casks with copper-pot-still tequila aged in ex-bourbon barrels, and thereby push the boundaries of what extra-añejo tequila can be.

Glycerine | ADDITIVE

A colourless, odourless and sweet-tasting liquid that is widely used in the food industry. Glycerine, also known as glycerol, has about 60 percent of the sweetening power of sugar, and as a humectant it helps substances retain moisture. In beverages, glycerine also increase viscosity. In Mexico, glycerine is an allowable additive for all categories of tequila except for blanco tequila. Glycerine can be added to a tequila to soften the effect of the alcohol on the palate, improve mouthfeel and add sweetness to the spirit. Glycerine can be derived from plant sources such as soya beans and palm oil as well as from animal products such as tallow.

Gold | CLASSIFICATION

Also referred to as joven (young), gold (or oro) tequila is a legal term defined by Mexico as a spirit derived from a fermented must of not less than 51 percent blue agave that may be mellowed and have its alcohol strength adjusted by dilution with water. Mellowing refers to the process of adding caramel colouring, oak extract, glycerine and/or sugar-based syrup. Gold tequila may also be produced by blending silver tequila with reposado (rested) or añejo (aged) tequila. In practice, most gold tequilas are mixtos (51 percent agave, 49 percent sugar-cane spirit) that get their golden hue from the addition of caramel colouring and which are smoothed out with the addition of glycerine or sugar syrup. Well-known examples are Jose Cuervo Especial Gold Tequila and Sauza Gold Tequila. Generally, gold tequilas are value products that are mostly used for mixing in tall drinks with soda or for making a batch of inexpensive Margaritas for parties.

SEE ALSO

Jose Cuervo *p138*

Normas Oficiales Mexicanas
(NOM) *p171*

Gran Centenario | BRAND

Lazaro Gallardo, a contemporary of Jose Cuervo and Cenobio Sauza, began producing tequila for his tavern in 1858. Near the beginning of the 20th century, Gallardo began selling his tequila and named it Centenario to mark the beginning of the new century. In 1920, Gallardo's son Luciano began bottling the tequila and selected a package and label inspired by Art Deco. At some point, Centenario was purchased by the Jose Cuervo company and, in 1996, the newly branded Gran Centenario replaced Cuervo's Dos Reales Tequila sold in the USA and Centenario Tequila sold in Mexico. Today, the tequila is made at Casa Cuervo (NOM 1122). The piñas are cooked with an autoclave and then pressed with a roller mill. The must is fermented in stainless-steel tanks and distilled using a column still. All of the Gran Centenario tequilas are aged for some amount of time and bottled at 40% ABV. The plata tequila is rested in oak for seven weeks, the reposado is matured for four months and the añejo is aged for sixteen months, all in new American oak barrels

SEE ALSO

Alambique *p22*

Double distilled *p94*

Normas Oficiales Mexicanas
(NOM) *p171*

Gran Dovejo | BRAND

Created in 2009 by Frank Mendez and his cousin Gran Dovejo, is made at Feliciano Vivanco y

Asociados (NOM 1414) in Los Altos de Jalisco by the Vivanco family. Gran Dovejo is designed to be an additive-free tequila that expresses the pure character of the blue agave. The estate-grown piñas are cooked for 36 hours in brick ovens and pressed with roller mills to separate the agave juices from the fibres. The cooked agave juice is fermented without the fibres using champagne yeast as classical music is played throughout the distillery. The fermented must is then double distilled in copper pot stills. The blanco is unaged, the reposado is matured between six and twelve months in re-charred bourbon barrels, while the añejo spends between eighteen and thirty-six months also in re-charred bourbon barrels. The aged expressions are barrelled around 43% ABV, which allows the alcohol to extract sweetness and flavour from the barrel without a lot of woody oak tannins.

Grand Marnier | BRAND

A liqueur made with cognac and sugar and flavoured with bitter oranges from the Caribbean. In 1880, Louis-Alexandre Marnier had the idea to make a curaçao using cognac as a base as opposed to a neutral spirit. But, when César Ritz, founder of the Ritz Hotel, tasted Marnier's curaçao, he exclaimed that it needed "a grand name for a grand liqueur!", hence Grand Marnier. In 1892, Louis-Alexandre Marnier trademarked the distinctive bottle he used for his liqueur, modelled after a cognac still and sealed with a red ribbon and wax. Then, in 2016, Gruppo Campari purchased the parent company of Grand Marnier for $759 million. Similar to Campari, Grand Marnier started off as a digestif, consumed neat or with ice. However, when Grand Marnier was used as a cocktail ingredient, the brand's popularity exploded. Grand Marnier adds a high-class twist to any cocktail that calls for an orange liqueur, curaçao or triple sec, such as a Margarita, Picador or Tequila Daisy.

SEE ALSO
Cabo Wabo *p51*
Campari *p53*
Espolòn *p104*
Grand Marnier *p117*
Normas Oficiales Mexicanas
(NOM) *p171*

Gruppo Campari | BRAND

Founded by Gaspare Campari in 1860, Campari started the company producing his eponymous aperitif as well as several other liqueurs, cordials and bitters. After Campari's passing in 1882, his son Davide grew the company, building its first production facility in Milan in 1904 and streamlining its portfolio to focus on its core products: Campari Bitter, Cordial Campari and the ready-to-drink Campari Soda. In 1995, Campari decided to expand its portfolio outside of Italian liqueurs and join the ranks of the world's leading spirit companies. In 2007, Gruppo Campari entered the tequila market with the purchase of Cabo Wabo Tequila, created by Sammy Hagar, former lead singer of Van Halen. Two years later, Campari also purchased the Espolòn tequila brand as well as the San Nicolas Distillery (NOM 1440), where both Espolòn and Cabo Wabo are made today.

SEE ALSO
Denomination of Origin for
Tequila (DOT) *p83*
Normas Oficiales Mexicanas
(NOM) *p171*

Guanajuato | REGION

Located in central Mexico, Guanajuato is one of Mexico's 31 states. The state is bounded to the south by the Trans-Mexican Volcanic Belt, while much of the rest of the state sits on the Central Mexican Plateau, which is an arid and semiarid region that averages 1,825m (5,988ft) above sea level. Historically, the state's economy has been driven by mining, agriculture and livestock, though today much of the economy is driven by

automobile production, processed foods and leather goods. Guanajuato is also one of five Mexican states included in the Denomination of Origin for Tequila (DOT). Tequila can be produced in seven western municipalities of Guanajuato that border the state of Jalisco. Tequila brands produced in the state include Ayate (NOM 1519), Huani 1875 (NOM 1593) and Real de Penjamo (NOM 1434).

Guerrero | REGION

SEE ALSO
Denomination of Origin for
Mezcal (DOM) *p80*

Named after Vicente Guerrero, a leader in the Mexican War of Independence (1810–21) and the second President of Mexico, the state of Guerrero is in south-west Mexico on the Pacific Ocean. Guerrero is a mountainous state and most of its economic activity comes from tourism. Despite this important economic engine, Guerrero is the number-one source of Mexican migrants to the USA as well as Mexico's leading producer of heroin. One potential bright spot is that, as the popularity of mezcal continues to increase, growing agave and producing mezcal might become a profitable alternative for rural farmers in the state. In 2016, Guerrero produced about 1 million litres (just over 264,000gal [US]) of mezcal, although only a few of the region's brands such as Mayalen and Mezcales de Leyenda export out of Mexico.

Gusano de maguey (maguey worm) | ADDITIVE

SEE ALSO
Agave *p16*
Sal de gusano *p207*

Two kinds of edible larvae can be found feasting on agave plants. The white maguey worm, *Aegiale hesperiaris*, is known as the *meocuil* in Spanish and the tequila giant skipper in English. In its caterpillar stage the larvae bore into the heart of the maguey where the plant stores most of its energy. The other, a red worm, the *chilocuil* or *Comadia redtenbacheri*, also infests the heart of the agave and makes its way to the root system, killing the plant. *Chilocuiles* have been used as a food source by the indigenous people of Mexico for thousands of years, and they can still be found fried and for sale in Oaxaca. A 100g (3½oz) serving of *chilocuiles* can contain up to 650 calories and is a good source of protein and fat. In the 1950s, the mezcal brand Gusano Rojo began adding a *chilocuil* to each bottle as a marketing tactic. In short order, a number of mezcal brands followed suit. However, today the worm in the bottle is seen as a gimmick and associated with low-quality mezcals.

H

Heads (*cabeza*) | PRODUCTION

A common name for the first chemical
compounds to come out of the still during
distillation. The heads are traditionally
comprised of the lightest compounds such
as acetone and methanol, which are toxic
for human consumption. During the second
distillation on a pot still or passing through
a column still, the heads are collected and
removed from the hearts, the portion of the
spirit comprised mostly of alcohol, water
and esters. The heads can be sold off for other
industrial purposes or used as a cleaning agent
in the distillery. There is a claim that, owing
to the particular chemistry of agave, when it is
being distilled, methanol bonds with some other
compound present in the still, which causes most
of the methanol to come out during the tails (the
end of the distillation process) rather than the
heads. Because of this, some mezcal producers
will use a portion of the heads, rather than water,
to adjust the alcohol concentration. Normally,
this would be rather alarming because methanol
poisoning attacks the optic nerve and can make
a person go blind. But all mezcal certified by the
CRM is guaranteed to have no more than 300mg
of methanol per 100ml, which is deemed to be in a
safe range for human consumption.

Hearts (*corazon*) | PRODUCTION

The beverage portion of a spirit that is saved
for bottling or put into a barrel for ageing.
Traditionally, as the spirit is coming off a pot
still during the second distillation, the aroma,
flavour and alcohol concentration will transform
to a more pleasant experience. This indicates
to the distiller that it is time to start collecting
the hearts to save for later. In more modern
operations, making the cut from heads to the
hearts can be made by watching the ABV. In
column stills, the vapours separate through the
height of the still depending on the weight of the
chemical compounds. The still is equipped with
collection points at different heights to separate
the heads, hearts and tails. All of these practices
apply to agave spirits, and separating the heads
from the rest of the distillation can have a
significant impact on the quality of the spirit. If
heads are left in the spirit, it can smell of nail-
polish remover. If too much of the tails are left in,
the spirit can taste hot and harsh in the mouth.

Hijuelos | PLANT

Also referred to as pups, hijuelos are agave
shoots that grow from the base of a mature agave
plant. Like clones, hijuelos are exact genetic
copies of the mother plant but already contain
a root system that can be used for replanting.
Hijuelos are essentially a failsafe reproduction
plan should the mother plant fail to flower and
produce seeds. There are a number of scenarios
in which an agave plant may not produce seeds:
a person or animal could damage or remove
the quiote; a significant amount of rain as the
quiote flowers could prevent many of the seeds
from pollinating; or a lack of pollinators in the

area could prevent the seeds from developing. Because the agave spends its whole life cycle preparing to seed before it dies, the plant has evolved a secondary strategy should the primary strategy fail.

Holm oak (*Quercus ilex*) | PLANT

SEE ALSO
French oak *p108*
White oak *p241*

A large evergreen species of oak native to the Mediterranean region. In Spanish, holm oak is known as encina and is prevalent from Portugal to Italy. Holm oak is a hardwood that is tough and can be used for construction, tools and even barrels for holding wine or spirits. Holm oak has a coarse grain, so it is likely that spirits stored in barrels made from holm oak would pick up a lot of flavour. In Spain, holm oak was used to make very large vats or barrels to store wine. Because of their size, the impact of the wood on the wine was diminished, so it may be possible that the Mexican regulations that explicitly allow holm oak to be used to store tequila reflect this tradition.

H

129

Hornitos | BRAND

SEE ALSO
Bagasse *p36*
Beam Suntory *p40*
Cristalino *p73*
Diffuser *p87*
Sauza Tequila *p211*

Created in 1950 by Francisco Javier Sauza, Hornito is now owned by Beam Suntory and currently sells over 1 million 9-litre (2.38gal [US]) cases per year. Hornitos is made using a diffuser and distilled with a column still. Some of the unaged tequila goes into the brand's Hornitos Plata or flavoured tequila, while the rest goes into barrels for its aged expressions. The reposado spends two months in large oak vats, while the añejo spends one year in oak barrels. From the añejo, Hornito also makes its Cristalino tequila, which takes one-year-old tequila and then carbon-filters out the colour.

Lastly, the Hornitos Black Barrel takes añejo
tequila, finishes it for four months in charred
American whiskey barrels, and then lets it rest
for two months in toasted oak barrels.

SEE ALSO
Autoclave *p30*
Bagasse *p36*
Brick oven *p49*

Horno | PRODUCTION

A traditional earthen pit oven used to slowly
roast agave. In the bottom of the pit, large chunks
of hardwood are stacked and set on fire. Once
the fire is fully lit, the wood is covered by a layer
of rock that helps retain the heat once the fire
has gone out. The rocks are then covered with
bagasse, which acts as a barrier to prevent the
piñas from burning through direct contact with
the fire or red-hot rocks. Once the bagasse is
laid, the piñas are stacked around the central
fire with the largest piñas on the bottom. Once
all the piñas are stacked in the horno, they are
covered with bagasse, palm leaves or some other
organic material. Then a tarpaulin is spread
over the bagasse/leaves and then is itself covered
with dirt. The piñas are then left for five days to
slowly cook, converting the inulin to fermentable
sugars. Cooking the agave with a horno can
impart a smoky flavour, depending on the type
of wood used and how the fire is managed. This is
why some ancestral and artisanal mezcals have a
particularly smoky taste.

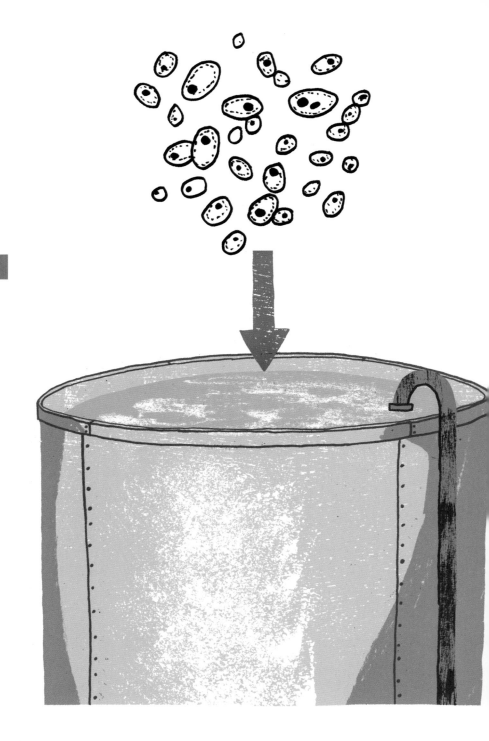

I

Inoculation | PRODUCTION

The process of adding a yeast culture to the fermentation vessel. Today, most breweries, wineries and distilleries use a specific yeast culture to ferment the available sugars. This yeast becomes part of what gives each spirit its signature flavour and aroma. Inoculating a new must with yeast helps prevent wild yeast and other microorganisms from taking control of the fermentation process and producing off flavours or aromas. Unlike using a natural fermentation, inoculating a must gives the distiller a predictable fermentation time, an expected attenuation (how much sugar gets converted to alcohol) and a flavour profile. Mexican regulations allow all agave spirits to be inoculated with cultivated yeast.

Inulin | PLANT

A soluble fibre found in agave (and in some 36,000 other plant species) that acts as a plant's primary store of chemical energy. In 1804, German scientist Valentin Rose discovered a substance while he was boiling *Inula helenium* roots in water, which he named inulin. Today, we know that inulin is essentially a long chain of fructose molecules that are water soluble. Because of this, when agaves are harvested for making spirits,

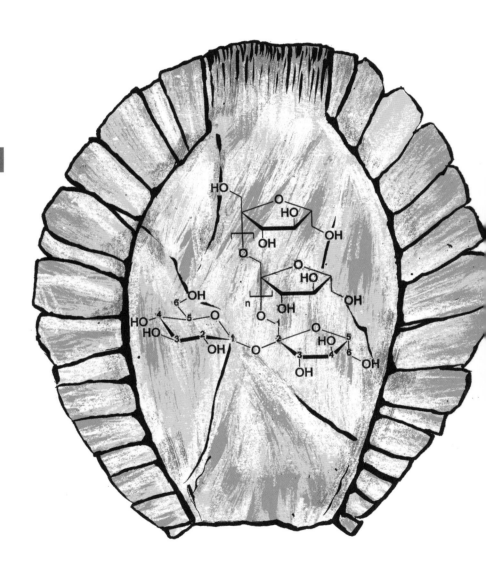

the inulin is converted into fructose, glucose and sucrose through a process called hydrolysis. In traditional ovens, steam heat generated from the piñas or injected into the oven liquefies the inulin and breaks the chains into smaller fermentable sugar molecules. In a diffuser, the inulin is liquefied by spraying the agave fibres with hot water. That water is then collected and heated in an autoclave, which breaks the inulin bonds into smaller sugars.

Jalisco | REGION

One of Mexico's 31 federal states, Jalisco extends from the Pacific Ocean eastward to the state of San Luis Potosí. Jalisco has 125 municipalities, and Guadalajara, a city of 1.4 million residents, is its capital. Jalisco is ranked as the third most economically productive state in Mexico and is known for producing tequila as well as for mariachi and ranchera music. The name Jalisco is derived from the Nahuatl word *xalisco*, which means "over a sandy surface". In 1530, the town of Tequila was established, and within one year a still had been erected and Spanish residents were using it to produce a spirit from aguamiel. By 1608, the governor of the Spanish colony of New Galicia, which covered parts of present-day Jalisco, introduced the first tax on "mezcal wine". In the 1940s, tequila became an official spirit of Jalisco, and it was not until 1974 that other regions outside of Jalisco were allowed to call their agave spirit tequila.

Jimador | PRODUCTION

A worker who harvests agaves wielding the long-handled hoe with a rounded blade called a coa de jima. The jimador is a skilled worker who, through long days in the fields, learns how to identify mature agave and harvest them quickly while removing only the necessary amount of the pencas (agave leaves). Historically, the knowledge of the jimador was passed from father, to son, to grandson, but in modern times gaps have begun to appear in this generational chain of knowledge. Economics, cartels and a general population trend from the country to the cities have sent many of the sons of jimadors into larger cities in Mexico or north to the USA to find better opportunities than backbreaking labour. However, jimadors play a very important role in the production of tequila and, in 1994, Tequila Herradura launched a 100 percent agave tequila called El Jimador in their honour.

SEE ALSO
Don Jose Antonio de Cuervo
p91

Jose Cuervo | BRAND

The world's largest tequila brand: in 2017, Jose Cuervo sold 9.5 million 9-litre (2.38gal [US]) cases. While the Cuervo family has been making tequila since the middle of the 1700s, it was only in 1900 that the spirit was named Jose Cuervo to honour the 18th-century family patriarch Don Jose Antonio de Cuervo. This same year, the primary Cuervo distillery was renamed La Rojeña, and the distillery still bears this name today. Over time, Jose Cuervo has expanded its bottlings, and today it produces seven different brands: 1800 Tequila, Azul Centenario, Maestro Dobel, Gran Centenario, Jose Cuervo Tradicional and Reserva de la Familia, all made with 100 percent agave, as well as Jose Cuervo Especial, a mixto tequila. In addition to distilling tequila, Jose Cuervo is also one of the single largest growers of agave, with millions of plants under cultivation.

Joven

See "Gold" (page 113).

Juan Collins | COCKTAIL

A tequila variation of the classic Tom Collins. The Collins family of cocktails is a group of tall drinks that have been popular since the middle of the 19th century. All Collins drinks contain sugar, lemon, spirit and soda water.

SEE ALSO
Agave syrup *p19*
Lemon *p145*

JUAN COLLINS RECIPE

45 ML / 1½ FL OZ BLANCO TEQUILA
30 ML / 1 FL OZ LEMON JUICE
15 ML / ½ FL OZ AGAVE SYRUP
SODA WATER

Fill a Collins glass with ice and add tequila, lemon juice and agave syrup. Stir to mix, top with soda water and garnish with a lemon slice.

Juárez Tequila | BRAND

SEE ALSO
Consejo Regulador del
  Tequila *p71*
Mixto *p163*
Normas Oficiales Mexicanas
  (NOM) *p171*

Owned by Luxco, based in St Louis, Missouri, Juárez Tequila is a mixto that is currently the fourth largest-selling value brand in the United States. Found mostly as a less expensive, "well" tequila for bars and restaurants, Juárez is currently made at Destiladora González González (NOM 1143) in Los Altos de Jalisco. Juárez starts with piñas cooked in autoclaves and then pressed with roller mills. The must is mixed with 49 percent sugars from other sources, most likely from cane, and then fermented. The mixto ferment is distilled in stainless-steel pot stills with copper coils. Juárez Tequila has two expressions – a silver (unaged mixto) bottled at 40% ABV and a gold tequila that is most likely coloured with spirit caramel and bottled at 40% ABV. In January 2017, a USA court sided with the

Consejo Regulador del Tequila (CRT) against Luxco, ruling that its flavoured neutral spirit mixed with tequila could not be marketed as tequila because it did not conform to the rules established by the Mexican government. In April of that year, Luxco announced that it had completed construction of its own distillery in Jalisco, allowing it to continue selling its tequila brands with real tequila in the bottles.

Kosher tequila | PRODUCTION

A tequila that has been certified by one of the
kosher certifying agencies means that it was
made in accordance with Jewish dietary laws.
While most tequilas would qualify as kosher, one
must pay to have a rabbi inspect the production
process and bottling to see whether it complies
with Jewish food laws. It is possible for a tequila
to be disqualified from receiving a kosher
certification if the producer has used non-
kosher yeast, or if the spirit has been mellowed
by the addition of glycerine or oak extract.
This means that many mixto tequilas as well as
many ancestral and artisanal mezcals would
not qualify as kosher. However, if a producer
receives a certification, then their product is
able to enter the kosher food market – currently
a $24-billion industry, and growing.

K
143

Lemon (*Citrus limon*) | COCKTAIL INGREDIENT

A citrus fruit that grows from a flowering evergreen tree. Lemon skins are oily and aromatic, and the tart juice has between 5 and 6 percent citric acid with a pH of about 2.2. The aromatics, flavour and tartness pair very well with the flavours and aromatics of tequila. Lemon peel or slices of the fruit are commonly used as a garnish, while the juice is used in a variety of cocktails. Genetic study of lemons has shown them to be a hybrid of the bitter orange (*Citrus aurantium*) and the citron (*Citrus medica*) developed in Asia somewhere between India and China. Lemons arrived in Europe sometime around the 2nd century AD and eventually spread to the Americas. Today, the Eureka lemon is the most common variety sold commercially because the plant flowers year round. Because of this, Eureka lemons are the most common variety used in cocktails and as garnish.

Lime | COCKTAIL INGREDIENT

Like other citrus fruits, the aroma, flavour and acidity of limes pair well with agave spirits, and it is not uncommon to find lime used as a garnish or the juice used to add acidity to a cocktail. What we know as limes are not just one fruit, but a variety of citrus produced mostly through hybridization. The three most popular limes in terms of cultivation are the makrut lime (*Citrus hystrix*), the Key lime (*C. x aurantiifolia*) and the Persian lime (*C. x latifolia*). The Persian lime, a hybrid created by crossing a Key lime and a lemon, is the most common lime variety grown because of its resistance to frost and wide habitable zone. While Mexico is the largest commercial grower of Persian limes, Key limes are more popular for domestic consumption in the country. The consequence of this is that while in many countries tequila cocktails using lime are made with Persian limes, tequila cocktails made in Mexico use Key limes.

Madurado en vidrio | CLASSIFICATION

A regulated term that refers to a practice of "maturing" mezcal in glass containers. In order to use the term, a mezcalero must let the spirit rest in a glass container, usually a demijohn or carboy, for more than 12 months, either underground, or in a space with minimal fluctuations in light, temperature and humidity. While some mezcal is matured using oak barrels, adding both flavour and colour from the barrel, maturing a spirit in glass works because glass is air permeable, thus allowing the spirit to slowly oxidize. Over time, this can break down harsh compounds into smaller components, softening the spirit and adding complexity without adding colour or wood flavour.

Maguey

See "Agave" (page 16).

Margarita | COCKTAIL

The earliest claim for the invention of the Margarita is from 1938, although in 1937 a drink called the Picador with the same ingredients and proportions can be found in the *Café Royal Cocktail Book* by W. J. Tarling, President of the United Kingdom Bartenders' Guild. It seems most likely that the Margarita and the Picador were independently invented as a variation on the Sidecar (brandy, orange liqueur and lemon). While the exact origin of the Margarita is shrouded in mystery, the first published recipe for the cocktail appeared in the December 1953 issue of *Esquire* magazine, and since then the drink has become the single most popular cocktail in the USA. The Margarita has produced a near-infinite number of variations, although the most notable are the Frozen Margarita, which turns the drink into an alcoholic slush, and the Tommy's Margarita, which was invented by Julio Bermejo in the early 1990s at Tommy's Mexican Restaurant in San Francisco. This variation substitutes the orange liqueur with a smaller portion of agave syrup, which allows the tequila to take centre stage.

MARGARITA RECIPE

30 ML (1 FL OZ) TEQUILA
15 ML (½ FL OZ) ORANGE LIQUEUR
15 ML (½ FL OZ) LIME JUICE

Combine in a cocktail shaker with ice and shake until cold. Strain into a rocks glass filled with ice or into a chilled stemmed cocktail glass garnished with a lime wedge and a salted rim.

SEE ALSO
Overharvesting *p178*

Market share | STATISTICS

Interest and enthusiasm in agave spirits, particularly in tequila, are growing rapidly around the world. The USA is the single largest consumer of tequila, currently purchasing around 17 million 9-litre (2.38gal [US]) cases per year, which accounts for about half of all tequila sold. Mexico is currently the second largest consumer of tequila, followed by China, Germany, Canada, Brazil, the UK and Japan. However, it is expected that in the very near

future China will supplant Mexico as the second largest consumer of tequila. Most of the growth in tequila of the last ten years has been among 100 percent agave tequilas, especially those produced by premium and higher-end brands. In the USA, in the 15 years from 2002, super-premium tequilas (those priced between $35 and $74.99) grew by 805 percent in sales. And while tequila has represented about 7 percent of the total US spirits market in recent years, its meteoric rise is likely to push that number even higher.

SEE ALSO
Centzon Totochtin *p58*

Mayahuel | HISTORY

An Aztec goddess of fertility and the maguey (agave plant). A lesser deity in the Aztec pantheon, Mayahuel was said to be have been held captive in the heavens by her jealous grandmother, Tzitzimitl, of the Tzitzimimeh, goddesses of the stars, who came to Earth during solar eclipses to devour humans. Quetzalcoatl, the feathered serpent god of creation and the wind, fell in love with Mayahuel, and together they escaped to Earth to hide from Tzitzimitl as a joined tree. Enraged that Mayahuel had escaped, Tzitzimitl found her and Quetzalcoatl, split the two apart and allowed the Tzitzimimeh to cook and devour the body of Mayahuel. Quetzalcoatl took the remains of his lover and buried her in the ground, from which the first maguey plant grew. In her new form as a maguey, Mayahuel provided humans with pulque, an alcoholic drink made from the fermented sap of the agave. In surviving Aztec codices, Mayahuel is depicted as springing from a maguey with 400 breasts with which to feed her children, the Centzon Totochtin ("400 Rabbits"), deities of mirth and drunkenness.

Mezcal (*mescal*) | CLASSIFICATION

Mexican regulation defines mezcal as a distilled spirit produced from 100 percent mature agave, harvested within the Denomination of Origin zone for Mezcal (DOM), cooked and fermented with either naturally occurring (wild) yeast or cultivated yeast. The regulation goes on to say that the aroma and flavour of mezcal should reflect the species of maguey used, the terroir from where it came, the process of cooking, fermentation and distillation employed in production, and the imprint of the mezcalero who oversaw production. In 2016, the regulations of mezcal were updated to include three categories of mezcal differentiated by how they are made. Spirits labelled as mezcal must be bottled between 35% and 55% ABV and can use modern techniques, such as cooking the piñas with an autoclave, using a mechanical shredder or diffuser to break apart the agave after cooking, fermenting in stainless-steel tanks, and using a stainless-steel column still for distillation. And, unlike tequila, one is allowed to blend mezcals only of the same category and type – that is, joven mezcal artisanal with joven mezcal artisanal, and so on.

Mezcal ancestral | CLASSIFICATION

A new category of mezcal, codified in the 2016 update to the regulations governing mezcal (NOM-070-SCFI), to protect and add value to the most ancient methods for mezcal production. As will all mezcal, ancestral mezcal must be made from 100 percent mature agave, grown in the Denomination of Origin region for Mezcal (DOM) and bottled between 35% and 55% ABV. In addition, ancestral mezcal can use only piñas

M
155

cooked with wood in an horno (earthen oven), milled using a mallet or a tahona after cooking, fermented in a container made from stone, earth, wood, clay, masonry or animal hides, and distilled with a direct-fired pot still made of clay. It is also allowed for the mezcalero to include the bagasse (agave fibres) during fermentation and distillation, if desired. This is a traditional practice in mezcal making, which some argue has a positive impact on the flavour profile of the final product.

Mezcal artesanal | CLASSIFICATION

Also codified in the 2016 update to NOM-070-SCFI regulating mezcal, artisanal mezcal protects and adds value for mezcals made using traditional techniques that have added some technological advances in distilling developed over the last hundred years or so, while excluding the most modern machinery and technology. As will all mezcal, artisanal mezcal must be made from 100 percent mature agave, grown in the Denomination of Origin region for Mezcal (DOM) and bottled between 35% and 55% ABV. Artisanal mezcal can use piñas cooked either in an horno (earthen oven) with wood or in a brick oven with indirect heat, milled using a tahona or a simple mechanical shredder, fermented in wooden vats – though stone, earth, clay, masonry or animal hide fermenters can also be used – and then distilled with a direct-fired pot still made from clay or copper. As with ancestral mezcal, artisanal mezcal is allowed to include the bagasse (agave fibres) during fermentation and distillation, if desired.

SEE ALSO
Tequila*p222*

Mezcal de tequila | HISTORY

Over the course of tequila's 400-year history, it has been known by a few different names. One of the earliest versions referred to the spirit as mezcal wine, the same as agave spirits made in other parts of Mexico. Then, in 1863, French writer Ernest Vigneaux identified the mezcal in regional terms when he noted: "Tequila [the Jaliscan town] lends its name to the mezcal liquor in the same way that Cognac [the town in the Charente] lends its name to the liquors of France." During the last half of the 19th century, tequila producers began to transition away from cooking the piñas in hornos, which gave the spirit a smokey flavour, to brick ovens, which cooked the agaves with indirect heat, giving it a cleaner taste. In 1893, mezcal de tequila was being regularly imported into the USA, and was entered into a competition and won an award during the Chicago World's Fair. Not long after this, the blue agave spirit from Jalisco came to be known simply as tequila.

SEE ALSO
Agavoni*p20*

Mezcal Negroni | COCKTAIL

As mezcal has grown in popularity, it did not take long for someone to try using mezcal – instead of the more commonly used gin – in a Negroni cocktail. Depending on the mezcal being used, the ultimate flavour of the drink can go in a number of different directions. One can pick a mezcal with more of a smoke-based character to play off the citrus, sweet and bitter elements to make an earthy and robust cocktail, or one can choose a more fresh/vegetal mezcal with little to no smoke character to make a more refreshing and bright drink.

M
159

30 ML / 1 FL OZ MEZCAL JOVEN
30 ML / 1 FL OZ CAMPARI
30 ML / 1 FL OZ SWEET VERMOUTH

Fill a mixing glass with ice and add equal parts of mezcal joven, Campari and sweet vermouth. Stir to mix, chill and dilute slightly. Strain into an Old Fashioned glass filled with ice and garnish with an orange twist. The drink can also be built in the glass: fill an Old Fashioned glass with ice, add all ingredients, stir to mix and garnish with an orange twist.

Mezcal Regulatory Council

See "Consejo Regulador del Mezcal" (page 68).

Michoacán | REGION

SEE ALSO
Denomination of Origin for
Mezcal (DOM) *p80*

M
160

A state divided into 113 municipalities, with its capital city, Michoacán, located at its centre. The name Michoacán comes from a Nahuatl phrase meaning "the place of fishermen". Michoacán was home to the Purépecha Empire, rival of the Aztec Empire. However, the empire was destroyed during the Spanish Conquest. Michoacán is in south-western Mexico and includes a portion of the Trans-Mexican Volcanic Belt. In addition, Mexico's two largest rivers, the Lerma and the Balsas, divide the state into three sections – North, Central and South. About 20 percent of the total land is used for agriculture; in addition to subsistence crops, Michoacán is the largest producer of avocados in the world. In 2006, Michoacán applied to include 30 of its municipalities within the Denomination of Origin for Mezcal (DOM), and after six years of review all 30 were then included on 22 November 2012.

Milagro | BRAND

Created by Danny Schneeweiss and Moises Guindi in 1997, Leyenda del Milagro aimed to create a tequila with an agave-forward flavour profile that at the time was lacking in the market. The piñas are cooked for 36 hours in brick ovens and pressed with a roller mill before the cooked agave juice is fermented without the fibres. The must is distilled once in a stainless-steel pot still and then in a stainless-steel column still. The unaged spirit is bottled as Milagro's silver tequila at 40% ABV. The reposado is matured in American oak barrels for three to six months, and the añejo is aged in the same type of barrels for fourteen to twenty-four months. Milagro also produce a second line of tequilas that are all matured in both American and French oak barrels. In 2006, William Grant & Sons purchased Milagro and built Tequilera Milagro (NOM 1559) in the southern Altos de Jalisco.

Mixto | CLASSIFICATION

While not a legally recognized term, mixto tequila is a common term used among aficionado and those interested in spirits to differentiate tequilas made from 51 percent agave sugars versus 100 percent agave tequilas. Mixto tequilas were first legalized in 1964, and at that time the law required a minimum of 70 percent agave sugar, but this was subsequently dropped to 51 percent in 1970. Adding 49 percent sugar from other sources during fermentation reduces the production cost of mixto tequilas, which is why for many years brands such as Jose Cuervo Especial and Juarez have remained as some of the bestselling tequila brands. It is almost certain that any mixto tequila on the market today has been made using a diffuser, further reducing the cost of production. Officially, tequilas made with only 51 percent agave sugar are just labelled tequila, so if one wants to avoid purchasing a mixto, be sure to look for 100 percent agave on the label.

SEE ALSO
Population crash *p190*

Monocropping | PLANT

The agricultural practice of growing one crop, often using one variety of the plant, on the same land, year after year. Monocropping is practised because it is highly efficient and cost effective. If a farm devotes itself to monocropping, it can focus its investments in specialized equipment, personnel or technology that allows greater yield and higher productivity from the land. While monocropping has allowed food supply to keep pace with the growing population of the planet, there is an ecological cost to the practice. Monocropping can deplete the soil of nutrients and so require the use of chemical fertilizers. Also, planting only one crop on a farm or plantation makes it more vulnerable to pests and pathogens, which requires the use of pesticides, herbicides and fungicides to allow the monocrop to survive. Monocropping is unnatural, so it can take significant energy and economic inputs to be profitable. The cultivation of blue agave for tequila production is one example of monocropping that could result in population crash.

SEE ALSO
Natural fermentation *p167*
Piñas *p190*
Yeast *p245*

Must | PRODUCTION

A mixture of water, fermentable sugars and plant material, referred to as mosto or tepache in Mexico. After the piñas are cooked and broken apart, the liquid and fibres are put

into fermenters. Distillers who use natural fermentation will often let the must sit for a couple of days before adding more water and kick-starting the fermentation process. If a sugar solution is too concentrated, yeasts are not able to survive, which allows other microorganisms to begin breaking down the fibres and sugars more. For distillers using cultivated yeast, water and yeast are added to start the fermentation process. As the yeast eats the sugar, one by-product is carbon dioxide, which pushes the fibres to the top of the fermenter. This creates a cap and an anaerobic environment where the yeast can focus on converting the sugar to alcohol. In an aerobic environment, yeast will use the sugar as energy to multiply and create more yeast cells.

N

Natural fermentation | PRODUCTION

Fermentation that allows wild yeast and other microorganisms living in the distillery to ferment the sugars present in the cooked agave. While natural fermentation is a common practice in the boutique wine world, most brewers and distillers generally use cultivated yeast. In the world of agave spirits, tequila is generally fermented using a cultivated yeast. However, it is very common to find ancestral and artisanal mezcals made with natural fermentation. While natural fermentation is usually less efficient than using cultivated yeast, wine makers and mezcaleros like using it because they believe that it produces better flavours out of the agave and gives the drink a sense of terroir – that is, a taste more indicative of the area it is from than that of a homogenized industrial product.

Nayarit | REGION

One of the smallest of the Mexican states, Nayarit is located in west-central Mexico on the Pacific Ocean. Most of Nayarit's economy is based on agriculture, the raising of livestock and fishing, though the state has invested in building up its tourist economy by marketing the 200 miles of coastline as the "Riviera Nayarita".

Access to this resort area is connected via a short flight from Puerto Vallarta in Jalisco. Nayarit shares a border with Jalisco, and nine of Nayarit's southern municipalities are within the Denomination of Origin for Tequila (DOT). At the time of writing, Nayarit has only one tequila distillery in operation, Corporativo Destileria Santa Lucia (NOM 1173), which produces 33 different tequila brands.

Norma Bebidas Alcohólicas Sotol (Sotol Regulations) | LAWS

The Mexican regulations governing sotol (NOM-159-SCFI) were issued in June 2004, and at first glance they mirror those for tequila. Sotol is broken down into two basic categories: 100 percent pure sotol, fermented and distilled from 100 percent dasylirion, and sotol distilled from a fermented mix of 51 percent dasylirion sugars and 49 percent other sugars. Each of these categories can come in one of four types: blanco or silver sotol is unaged and can be diluted to bottling strength only with water; joven or gold sotol can either be aged one to two months in wood containers or be a mixture of blanco and reposado sotols; reposado sotol is matured between two and twelve months in containers made of oak, acacia, chestnut, beech, ash or with other technological alternatives (this term is undefined in the NOM); and añejo sotol is matured for a minimum of one year in containers no larger than 210 litres (about 55gal [US]) made of oak, acacia, chestnut, beech, ash or with other technological alternatives. Joven, reposado and añejo sotols may be mellowed with the addition of no more than 1 percent by weight of caramel colour, oak extract, glycerine and/or sugar syrup. If reposado or añejo sotols list a numerical

age, it represents the weighted average of the ages and volumes of their components. Lastly, sotols must be bottled between 35% and 55% ABV.

Normas Oficiales Mexicanas (NOM) | LAWS

SEE ALSO
Consejo Regulador del
  Mezcal *p68*
Consejo Regulador del
  Tequila*p71*

Often shortened to Normas or NOMs, these are the "Official Mexican Standards" by which all sorts of goods and services are regulated within Mexico. Regulations for all alcoholic beverages can be found in NOM-199-SCFI, and the specific regulation for tequila and mezcal can be found in NOM-006-SCFI and NOM-070-SCFI, respectively. While most NOMs are enforced by the appropriate federal agency in Mexico, the Mexican government has allowed two private organizations, the Consejo Regulador del Tequila (Tequila Regulatory Council) and the Consejo Regulador del Mezcal (Mezcal Regulatory Council) to oversee enforcement of the respective Normas for tequila and mezcal. Each bottle of tequila or mezcal certified by its respective council carries a NOM number (e.g. NOM-1493, NOM-O37X) identifying the distillery that produced the spirit.

North American Free Trade Agreement (NAFTA) | LAWS

The North American Free Trade Agreement (NAFTA) came into force in January 1994 and created a trilateral trading bloc between Mexico, Canada and the USA. NAFTA covered many areas of trade and commerce between the three countries, one of them being distilled beverages. Through the trade agreement, the USA, Canada and Mexico agreed to recognize a select number of beverages as protected spirits. These include

Canadian whisky, USA bourbon, Tennessee whiskey and Mexican tequila. Because the USA is the largest consumer of tequila, it was important for the tequila industry to secure that country's support in respecting tequila's Denomination of Origin (DO).

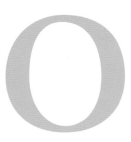

Oak

See "French oak" (page 108), "Holm oak" (page 129) and "White oak" (page 241).

Oak extract | ADDITIVE

A concentrated oak-flavoured tincture that may be added to all tequilas, except blanco tequila, as a mellowing agent. When added to tequila, oak extract can add pleasant wood flavours such as caramel, vanilla, coffee, cocoa, toast and roasted nuts as well as oak tannins that can add structure to the mouthfeel and dryness to the spirit. According to Mexican regulations, oak extract used in tequila may be derived from "natural" or "Encino", where "natural" refers to deciduous varieties of oak such as white oak or French oak, and Encino oak refers to evergreen varieties of oak such as holm oak. Oak extracts are made by combining oak dust with water and enzymes that are then heated. The heat activates a chemical process that causes enzymatic and thermal breakdown of the oak particles, dissolving the flavours and character of the wood into the water.

Oaxaca | REGION

One of the poorest states in Mexico, Oaxaca is in the south-west of the country and home to the

Mixtec, Zapotec and several other indigenous peoples. The geography of the state is largely shaped by the convergence of three mountain ranges, with the valleys in between forming the major population centres. Evidence of human activity in Oaxaca goes back to 11,000 BCE, and the discovery of the Guilá Naquitz Cave provided evidence of domesticated corn, squash and beans around 2000 BCE, as well as remnants of cooked agave for food. After Jalisco, Oaxaca is the second largest producer of agave and makes about 98 percent of all mezcal. Mezcal has played an important role in the cultural life of Oaxacans since at least the Spanish colonial period, and has given birth to the saying, "Para todo mal, mezcal; para todo bien, también" (For everything bad, mezcal; for everything good, too). There are a few large industrial producers of mezcal in the state, with most being small, family-run operations.

SEE ALSO
Mayahuel *p152*

O

174

Oaxaca Old Fashioned | COCKTAIL

Created by bartender Phil Ward when working at the New York City cocktail bar Death & Co., the Oaxaca Old Fashioned was most likely not the first variant of the Old Fashioned to substitute an agave spirit for bourbon, but it has become the best known. Since the creation of this drink, Ward has opened his own bar called Mayahuel, located in New York's East Village.

OAXACA OLD FASHIONED RECIPE

45ML / 1½FL OZ REPOSADO TEQUILA
15ML / ½FL OZ MEZCAL JOVEN
1 BARSPOON (5ML) AGAVE SYRUP
2 DASHES ANGOSTURA BITTERS

In an Old Fashioned glass with one large ice cube, add all the ingredients and stir until chilled, then garnish with a flamed orange peel. To flame, take a 5cm (2in) strip of orange peel,

strike a match and gently warm the peel with the flame. Then express the orange oils over the glass while still holding the match between the glass and the peel. The oils will briefly ignite and then drop the peel into the glass. One variation of the Oaxaca Old Fashioned substitutes mole bitters for Angostura, adding a nice spicy, chocolate note to the drink.

Olla de barro | PRODUCTION

Also referred to as a Filipino still, olla de barro is a clay pot still used in Oaxaca and other parts of Mexico to produce traditional spirits. The clay pot still is built into a base of either earth or brick that allows a fire to be built underneath it; the base acts as an insulator, allowing the distiller to use less wood during the distillation process. Usually, the clay stills are filled with the entire must during the first distillation – water, agave fibres and all. A clay or wooden head is placed on top of the pot and sealed with bagasse. Inside the head is a suspended catch plate that funnels condensed spirit to the lyne arm and into a collection vessel. On top of the head sits a copper bowl filled with cold water. As the vapours rise from the still, they condense on the cold copper bowl and drip onto the catch plate and out to the collection vessel.

O

177

Orange | COCKTAIL INGREDIENT

Similar to the lemon and lime, oranges are commonly used in conjunction with tequila and other agave spirits. Orange zest or a slice of orange is used as a garnish, while orange juice can add sweetness and acidity to a cocktail. However, the most common use for orange in relation to tequila is as a flavoured liqueur such as triple sec, curaçao or Grand Marnier. Oranges come in two basic groups: bitter orange (*Citrus aurantium*), generally used as a flavouring agent, and sweet orange (*Citrus sinensis*), generally used for eating and juicing. In Oaxaca, when one orders a shot of mezcal, it is common for the drink to come paired with a small plate of orange slices and sal de gusano. And in the USA, the best-known marriage of orange and tequila comes in the form of the modern Tequila Sunrise, which combines tequila, orange juice and grenadine.

Orange bitters | COCKTAIL INGREDIENT

SEE ALSO
Agavoni *p20*

A one-time staple of the barman, found in punches and Martinis, orange bitters were almost extinct by the 1960s. In the USA, Fee Brothers, based in Rochester, New York, was the only commercial source of orange bitters for about 30 years. Then, in the early 2000s, new brands of orange bitters began to appear on the market. Almost all orange bitters use bitter orange (*Citrus aurantium*) as the main flavouring ingredient combined with cardamom, caraway seed and coriander in a high-proof alcohol base. While not a common ingredient in tequila cocktails, the Agavoni is a good example of where the bitters can add the desired flavour without also adding a significant amount of sugar as well.

Oro

See "Gold" (page 113).

Overharvesting | PLANT

SEE ALSO
Blue agave *p45*
Espadin *p103*

The practice of harvesting a plant or resource faster than it is being regrown or replanted. Since 2002, tequila consumption in the USA (the largest market for the agave spirit) has grown an average of 6 percent per year, selling about 90 million litres (about 23.75 million gal [US]) more in 2017 than in 2002. Because

of this demand – which shows no real signs of slowing, save for a potential trade war – both the tequila and the mezcal industries have been overharvesting agave since about 2014. Because there is money to be made for workers, farmers, distillers and brand owners, no one seems to be slowing production but rather increasing it, exacerbating the overharvesting. In tequila, diffuser technology has allowed those companies to produce tequila from both mature and immature plants, which will make the current shortage of ripe agave worse in the next few years. And, although tequila can be made only from blue agave, there have been persistent rumours that truckloads of espadin from Oaxaca and other states are being smuggled into Jalisco to make it. In mezcal, success has been even more of a problem. Many mezcaleros rely on wild agave for their mezcal, but in the five years from 2012 to 2017, production grew by 1,000 percent. And while some mezcal distilleries are actively replanting agave, even from seed, so far no one is replanting more than are being harvested. There is a real danger that some wild varieties of agave that do not respond well to cultivation may go extinct due to overharvesting in the next couple of decades.

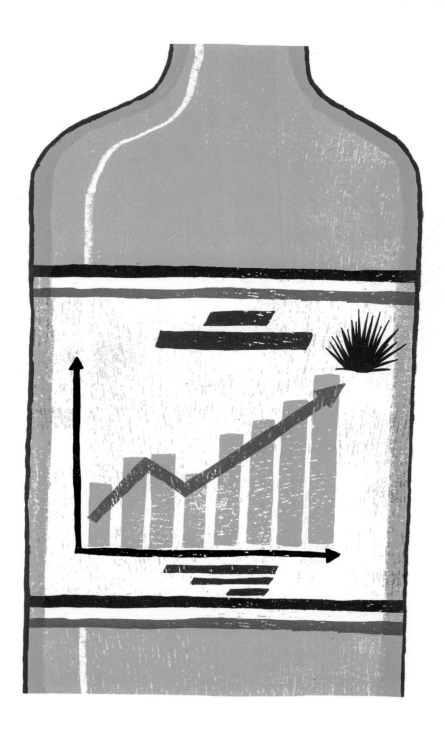

Paloma | COCKTAIL

One of the most popular tequila cocktails in Mexico, the Paloma, Spanish for "dove", is a tart and refreshing tall cocktail that combines tequila with grapefruit soda. One advantage of the drink's simplicity is that it can be easily made and remade with friends over a meal.

PALOMA RECIPE

60ML / 2FL OZ BLANCO TEQUILA
1 PINCH SALT
HALF A LIME
GRAPEFRUIT SODA

Fill a highball glass with ice and add the tequila, with a pinch of salt. Squeeze half a lime into the glass and drop into the drink for garnish, and top off with grapefruit soda. For a fresher variation, mix 60ml (2fl oz) both of tequila and grapefruit juice in a highball glass filled with ice, add 15ml (½fl oz) of lime juice and top off with soda water.

Partida | BRAND

Founded in 2004 by Sofia Partida and J Gary Shansby, Partida tequila is made with the blue agaves grown on the estate owned by Sofia's uncle. The agaves are cooked for nine hours in an autoclave and pressed with a roller mill. The cooked agave juices are fermented in stainless-steel tanks before being double distilled in stainless-steel pot stills. The Partida blanco is unaged and bottled at 40% ABV, while the reposado, añejo and extra añejo are aged in used Jack Daniel's barrels for six, eighteen and forty months, respectively. Today, Partida is produced at the Autentica Tequilera (NOM 1502) located in the Tequila Valley and is priced in as a premium spirit.

Patrón | BRAND

Founded in 1989 by John Paul DeJoria, of Paul Mitchell hair-care products, and Martin Crowley, Patrón was one of the first-ever super-premium tequilas and in 2017 sold 2.6 million 9-litre (2.38gal [US]) cases. Originally produced at Siete Leguas (NOM 1120), Patrón built its own distillery (NOM 1492), equipped with tahonas, roller mills and small copper pot stills. Despite Patrón's growing success and effective marketing, the owners considered the quality of the spirit to be more important than production efficiency. As the brand has grown, its master distiller, Francisco Alcaraz, has added more tahonas and more small pot stills rather than move to a diffuser and column still setup, which would be more cost effective but alter the flavour profile of the spirit. The Patrón silver is the brand leader, selling over 1 million cases. The Patrón reposado, añejo and extra añejo follow the regulation limits and are aged for two, twelve and thirty-six months, respectively. The Roca Patrón line is a higher-end product sold in silver (unaged), reposado (five months) and añejo (fourteen months) expressions. In addition, Patrón has an ultra-premium line called Gran Patrón as well as some flavoured tequilas. In 2018, Bacardi Ltd purchased Patrón for a reported $5.1 billion.

SEE ALSO
Bacardi Ltd *p35*
Cazadores *p58*
Normas Oficiales Mexicanas
(NOM) *p171*

P

184

Pechuga | CLASSIFICATION

Pechuga, which translates as "breast", refers to the practice of hanging a piece of meat such as a chicken, turkey, rabbit or lamb in the vapour path of the still to add flavour to the final spirit. While it is not known exactly how long this practice has existed, mezcal de pechuga has traditionally been reserved for major life celebrations such as baptisms and weddings. Pechugas also tend to include nuts, spices, dried fruit and grains to the still, making each pechuga unique to the mezcalero making it. Typically, a pechuga will start off with a twice-distilled mezcal made from espadin. The still is filled with mezcal and botanicals while the meat is hung in the vapour path of the spirit, which steams the meat, as opposed to stewing in the liquid. Despite the process, pechugas do not really taste like meat, the resulting flavour being more a combination of herbs and umami. Because pechugas are distilled three times, they are very expensive to make and to buy. For vegetarians or those put off by the idea of meat in their mezcal, there are some pechugas made with just mole spices or other combinations of botanicals.

P

187

Pencas (leaves) | PLANT

The leaves of an agave plant that help synthesize solar energy into inulin and act as a barrier to protect the heart of the plant, where most of the energy reserve is stored. For many traditional cultures, agricultural resources were not used solely for one purpose. In Mexico, all parts of the agave might be used. The heart of the plant could be used for pulque or roasted for food. The leaves of the agave are very fibrous, and people would use them to make rope or for weaving

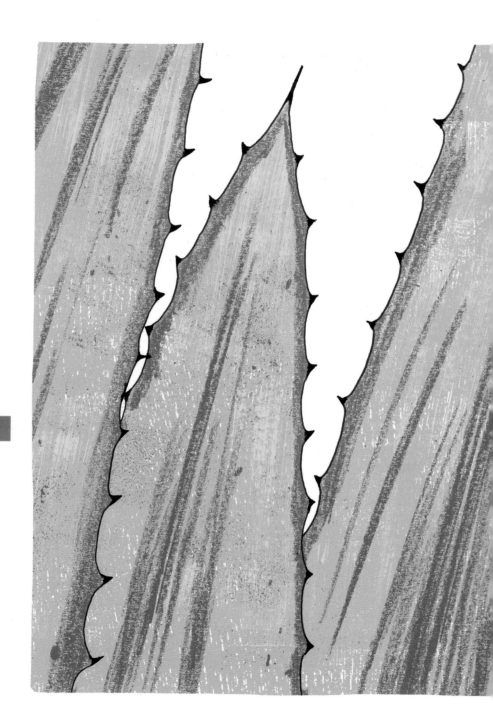

mats. In addition, the spines or thorns on the agave leaves were used as needles or hooks. In the pre-Columbian era, the Aztec and Maya peoples practised a variety of body modifications including piercings and scarification, and it is possible that they used the spines from agave plants for these rituals.

Pernod Ricard | BRAND

Founded in 1975, Pernod Ricard formed from the merger of two well-known producers of anise-flavoured spirits, and today Pernod Ricard is the world's second largest producer of distilled spirits. In 2000, Pernod purchased a little more than 38 percent of Seagram's portfolio when it went bankrupt. Part of the purchase included Destileria Colonial de Jalisco, founded in 1967 in the southern Altos de Jalisco, now called Pernod Ricard Mexico (NOM 1111), and the Olmeca tequila brand. Olmeca is made up of three distinct lines. The original is a mixto tequila that comes in blanco, gold, reposado, añejo and flavoured versions. In 2009, Pernod introduced Olmeca Altos, a 100 percent agave tequila made with piñas cooked in brick ovens, crushed with roller mills and a tahona, distilled in a copper pot and bottled as a plata, reposado and añejo. Then, in 2014, Pernod added Olmeca Tezón, a 100 percent agave, 100 percent tahona tequila, bottled as blanco, reposado and añejo. Pernod's presence in agave spirits grew when it bought a majority stake in Del Maguey Mezcal, followed in January 2018 by the acquisition of Avión Tequila.

P
189

Picador | COCKTAIL

First published by the Englishman William J. Tarling in the 1937 *Café Royal Cocktail Book*, the Picador is one of the oldest-known tequila cocktails and predates the Margarita. Named for the Spanish horseman who assists in bullfighting, the Picador is a spirit-forward cocktail that, like the Margarita, pairs tequila with orange liqueur and lime juice.

PICADOR RECIPE

60ML / 2FL OZ BLANCO TEQUILA
30ML / 1FL OZ ORANGE LIQUEUR
30ML / 1FL OZ LIME JUICE

Fill a cocktail shaker with ice and add all the ingredients. Shake until cold and strain into a chilled, stemmed cocktail glass. If desired, garnish with a lime twist.

SEE ALSO
Agave *p16*

Piña | PRODUCTION

The centre of an agave plant. When an agave is trimmed of its leaves, it reveals a round or oblong mass that resembles a pineapple, which is why in Spanish they are referred to as piñas. Depending on the variety of agave being harvested, piñas can range in weight of between 40 and 100kg (about 88–220lb) and have anywhere between 20 and 40 percent available sugars (also known as brix). The piñas will be stripped of their leaves and detached from their roots out in the field and then trucked to the distillery. There, depending on their size and the cooking method being used, the piñas may be halved or left whole.

Plata

See "Blanco" (page 43).

SEE ALSO
Bats *p39*
Clone *p62*
Monocropping *p164*

Population crash | PLANT

A sudden decline in the population of a species or group of organisms. A few times in human

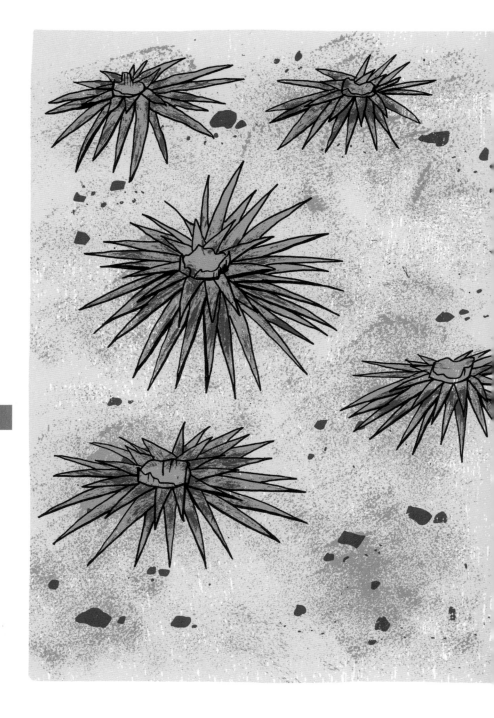

history there have been large-scale population crashes in food crops. In the 1800s, coffee rust wiped out most of the coffee grown in Ceylon (Sri Lanka), Africa and large parts of Asia. At the turn of the 20th century, fusarium wilt disease destroyed banana plantations throughout Latin America. Both of these crashes were caused by monocropping and cloning. Large areas of land were planted with one clone of one variety of plant because cloning desirable plants that produce good food crops is more profitable. However, they have little to no defence against new pathogens. Today, blue agave faces a similar potential for population crash because most blue agaves are cloned and monocropped in large plantations. Simple measures such as planting from seed and intercropping can reduce this threat. However, the economic cost of applying these measures has slowed their adoption.

Proofing | PRODUCTION

The process of adjusting the alcoholic concentration of a distilled spirit, usually with the addition of water. When a spirit comes off the still in its final run, the alcohol concentration is usually somewhere between 60% and 90% ABV. Once a spirit is ready for bottling, whether it is unaged or has been matured, it must be proofed down to bottling strength beforehand. The spirit will be put into a large tank and slowly the distiller will add water to bring down the ABV. If water is added too quickly, it can react with fatty acids in the spirit or from added glycerine, and create new compounds that smell like liquid hand soap! In some mezcal traditions, it is common to find distillers proofing their spirit with the addition of heads instead of water, which is a very unusual practice compared to the rest of the world.

Proximo Spirits | BRAND

Founded in 2007 by the Beckmann family, owners of Jose Cuervo, Proximo Spirits is a USA-based company that holds Jose Cuervo's USA assets and acts as its USA importer for its various international spirits. In addition to the Cuervo tequilas, Proximo also imports Mezcal Creyente from Oaxaca, Three Olives Vodka and Boodles Gin from the UK and Bushmills Irish Whiskey from Northern Ireland. In 2010, Proximo made its foray into USA craft spirits, with the purchase of Hangar 1 Vodka from California, followed one year later by Stranahan's Colorado Whiskey.

Puebla | REGION

Located in east-central Mexico, the city of Puebla was established in 1531 as a waypoint for trade between Mexico City and Veracruz on the Gulf of Mexico. Gradually, the territory controlled by the city increased, leading to the creation of Puebla State. Puebla is one of the most industrialized states in Mexico, but, because much of that development has been focused in the cities, the countryside has remained very poor and has been a significant source of migrants to Mexico City and the USA. Mostly situated on the Central Mexican Plateau, Puebla has a wide array of ecosystems from rainforest to arid zones covered in wild agave. In March 2017, 116 of Puebla's 217 municipalities were added to the Denomination of Origin for Mezcal (DOM), which at that time included 37 pre-existing brands. In addition to growing espadin, Puebla is also home to *Agave cupreata*, known locally as papalometl.

SEE ALSO
Natural fermentation *p167*
Quiote *p199*

Pulque | CLASSIFICATION

An ancient fermented beverage from
Mesoamerica, pulque is the fermented sap
of the agave plant, dating to about 200 AD.
Its name seems to derive from a Spanish
misunderstanding of the Nahuatl phrase octli
poliuhqui ("spoiled pulque"). During the Aztec
period, pulque was an important ritual drink for
priests, warriors and victims of human sacrifice,
but was also used to nourish the elderly, the sick
and nursing mothers and to celebrate important
events such as harvests, marriages, births
and burials. Post-Conquest, pulque remained
very popular, and at the beginning of the 20th
century, Mexicans consumed about 500 million
litres (over 132gal [US]) per year. To make
pulque, a tlachiquero (person who makes pulque)
selects a mature agave (usually *Agave salmiana*),
castrates the plant by removing the quiote bud
(flowering stalk) and then carves out a cavity in
the centre of the plant. The cavity fills with a sap
called *aguamiel* (honey water), which is collected
daily for up to six months, producing about 1,000
litres (about 265gal [US]) before the plant dies.
The collected *aguamiel* is allowed to ferment,
which produces a white, slightly acidic and
viscous drink of between 4% and 8% ABV.

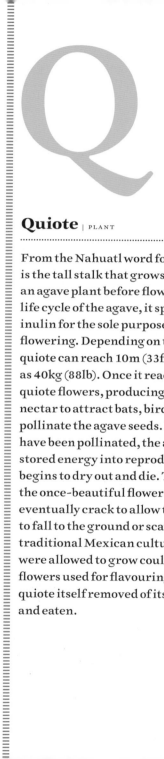

Quiote | PLANT

From the Nahuatl word for "stem", the quiote
is the tall stalk that grows from the centre of
an agave plant before flowering. During the
life cycle of the agave, it spends years storing
inulin for the sole purpose of reproducing via
flowering. Depending on the species of agave, the
quiote can reach 10m (33ft) and weigh as much
as 40kg (88lb). Once it reaches its full height, the
quiote flowers, producing blooms that are full of
nectar to attract bats, birds and other insects to
pollinate the agave seeds. By the time the seeds
have been pollinated, the agave has put all of its
stored energy into reproducing and the plant
begins to dry out and die. The quiote hardens and
the once-beautiful flowers turn into pods, which
eventually crack to allow the agave seeds within
to fall to the ground or scatter on the wind. In
traditional Mexican cultures, the quiotes that
were allowed to grow could be harvested, their
flowers used for flavouring specific foods and the
quiote itself removed of its outer layer, roasted
and eaten.

Q

Raicilla | CLASSIFICATION

According to Mexican regulation, raicilla is a regional distilled spirit made in Jalisco and Nayarit from 100 percent mature agave. The agave must be cooked, fermented with either wild or cultivated yeast, distilled and bottled between 35% and 55% ABV. Raicilla can be made from *Agave maximiliana, A. inaequidens, A. valenciana, A. angustifolia* (espadin) and *A. rhodacantha*, although it cannot be made from Weber blue agave. Other than that, there are no other rules governing raicilla, which gives the raicillero (the raicilla maker) a lot of flexibility. As an example, it is not uncommon for raicillas to be distilled only once as opposed to twice, as happens with tequila and mezcal. Translated as "little root", raicilla apparently gets its name from distillers trying to avoid paying their taxes by claiming that the spirit was distilled from roots rather than agave piñas. Because Jalisco is outside of the Denomination of Origin for Mezcal (DOM), raicilla cannot legally be called mezcal even though they are very similar.

Reposado | CLASSIFICATION

A regulated labelling term in Mexico as a nonspecific age statement for tequila and

mezcal. Reposado tequilas (mixto or 100 percent agave) must spend between two months and one year in an oak barrel or container that is no more than 600 litres (about 158gal [US]) in volume. While reposado translates as "rested", if a producer chooses to use an English translation of reposado on the label, it must say "aged". For mezcal, mezcal artesanal or mezcal ancestral to be labelled reposado, it must also spend between two and twelve months in a wooden container that has no limit on its size, shape or capacity but with the caveat that it must be stored in an area with minimal variations in light, temperature and humidity. As with añejo mezcal, there is no specification for the type of wood that can be used to create the container, leaving open the possibility to use other non-oak wood sources for its construction.

SEE ALSO
Caballito p51
Vaso veladora p239

Riedel tequila glasses | GLASSWARE

In 2001, the Riedel glassware company released the Ouverture tequila glass. Riedel, which is known for producing wine glasses with different shapes based on the style of wine or grape variety, took this same philosophy and began applying it to spirits. The Ouveture tequila glass is a machine-made stemmed crystal glass with a total volume of 190ccm (6¾oz) and a height of 210mm (8¼in). From its stem the glass flares out to its widest part and then chimneys upward with a slight taper toward the mouth. The glass was designed specifically with reposado tequilas in mind and intends to highlight the subtle agave notes on the nose and emphasize the soft and sweet flavours imparted into the spirit during its short maturation. In 2013, Riedel designed a "new" glass, the Vinum tequila glass, which has the same design as the Ouverture but is made

R

203

with lead crystal, which tends to give the glass more weight, better durability and more clarity.

Roller mill | PRODUCTION

A machine that presses cooked piñas to separate the agave fibres from the cooked juice. A roller mill usually consists of a staggered series of four or more conveyor belts at an incline with rollers at the top of each. The first conveyor belt carries chunks of cooked agave up to the first rollers, where the chunks are pressed and the juice is extracted and captured, while the fibres drop down to the second belt, where they are pressed again, and so on, until most of the moisture has been extracted from the fibres. The collected agave juice is then pumped in to tanks to begin fermentation, and the fibres (bagasse) are used as biofuel or for a number of other applications.

SEE ALSO
Bagasse *p36*
Diffuser *p87*
Egyptian mill *p99*
Tahona *p219*

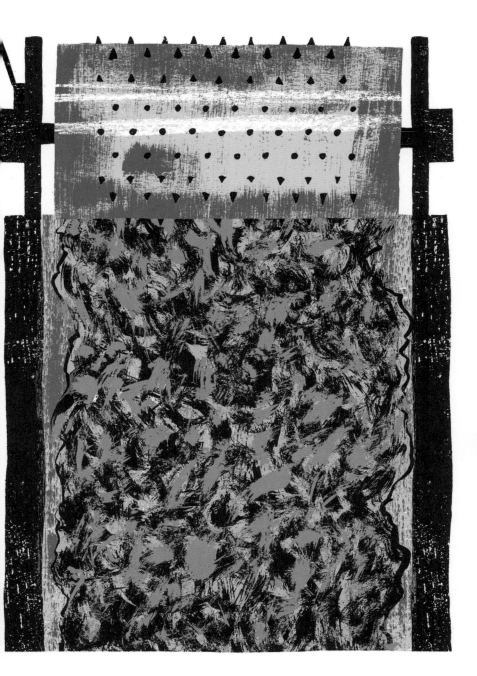

S

SEE ALSO
Gusano de maguey *p121*

Sal de gusano (worm salt)

COCKTAIL INGREDIENT

....

A spice mix made from a grinding together salt, dried chilli peppers and toasted red moth larvae, which are found on agave plants. In Oaxaca, and other parts of Mexico, sal de gusano is used as a spice to flavour food and is commonly served alongside fresh orange slices and a shot of mezcal. Sal de gusano has an earthy, smokey and umami flavour that pairs well with mezcal. Unlike the "lick of salt and bite of lime" ritual carried out to make cheap tequila palatable, taking a bite of an orange slice sprinkled with sal de gusano highlights and complements the flavours of mezcal rather than masking them. Insects such as crickets, caterpillars and moth larvae have been a staple source of protein and fat in the Mesoamerican diet for thousands of years, so it is no wonder that they were combined with salt to make a rich and flavourful seasoning. Today, owing to the growing popularity of mezcal, several companies are beginning to import sal de gusano into the USA to use in cooking and as a complement to agave spirits.

SEE ALSO
Bloody Maria *p43*
Margarita *p129*
Sal de gusano *p207*

Salt | COCKTAIL INGREDIENT

....

An essential element needed for human survival, salt has been used as a food preservative and flavour enhancer for millennia. As with food, salt has been used as a cocktail ingredient to enhance the flavours of a drink. Among tequila cocktails, the salted glass rim for a Margarita is by far the most famous. For many, taking a sip of the drink through the salty rim enhances the flavours of the Margarita and balances out the sweetness of the cocktail. In addition to the Margarita, salt is an important ingredient in the Bloody Maria, accentuating the tomato flavour that otherwise can taste flat and one-dimensional. Besides making foods and drinks taste good, salt serves an important metabolic function by helping the body retain water and enabling the nervous and muscular systems to function properly. That said, while some salt is necessary for a healthy body, there is evidence that for some people salt can increase blood pressure and put stress on the cardiovascular system.

SEE ALSO
Denomination of Origin for
Mezcal (DOM) *p80*

San Luis Potosí | REGION

Located in north-central Mexico, the city of San Luis Potosí was founded in 1592, after the discovery of nearby gold and silver deposits, and eventually gave its name to the surrounding region, one of Mexico's 32 states. In addition to mining and metallurgy, the economy of San Luis Potosí is supported by manufacturing and jobs in the service sector. Most of the state sits on the Central Mexican Plateau, which in the arid and semiarid regions can support growing wheat, corn, beans, cotton and agave, while the tropical southern valleys grow sugar, coffee, tobacco, peppers and fruit. One of the five original states included in the 1994 Denomination of Origin for Mezcal (DOM), San Luis Potosí was one of the largest producers of mezcal before the Mexican Revolution (*c.*1910–20). Post-revolution, land

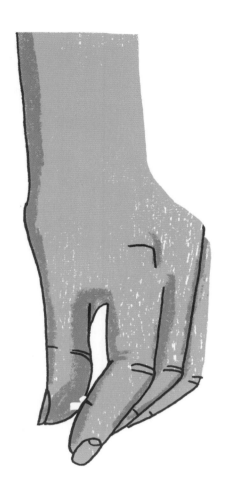

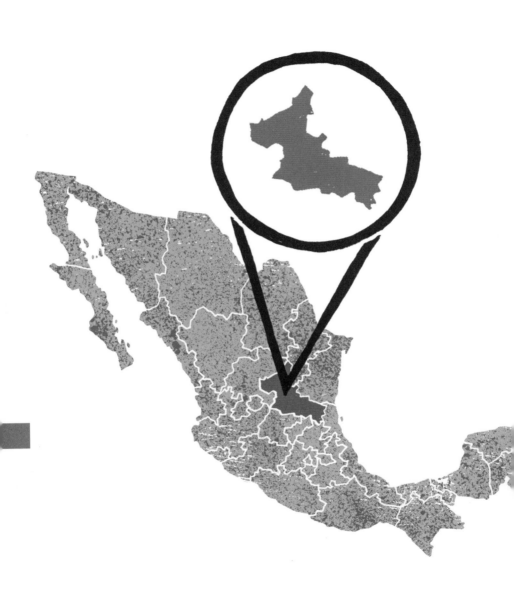

reform broke up many of the large haciendas, and this destroyed the industry. Today, the rising popularity of mezcal is reviving interest in mezcals from the state, some of which have done well in international competitions.

Sauza Tequila | BRAND

The second bestselling tequila worldwide, Sauza is currently selling just shy of 3 million 9-litre (2.38gal [US]) cases per year. Sauza Tequila was founded in 1873 when Don Cenobio Sauza opened his La Perseverancia distillery in Tequila, Mexico. That same year, Sauza also began exporting tequila to the USA. Sauza Tequila remained a family-owned company for over 100 years, until 1976, when Spanish brandy producer Pedro Domecq purchased it. Through a series of mergers and acquisitions, Sauza Tequila ended up in the hands of Beam Suntory, and while La Perseverancia distillery (NOM 1102) is still located in Tequila, its production processes have been modernized to maximize efficiency and achieve lower costs. Sauza was one of the first tequila producers to install a diffuser, which is much more efficient at extracting sugars from raw agave. The Sauza Tequila lineup includes silver, gold, reposado, añejo and flavoured tequilas as well as some ready-to-drink tequila cocktails. In addition to the Sauza tequila brands, the distillery also produces 100 Años, Hornitos and Tres Generaciones tequilas.

Siete Leguas | BRAND

Created in 1952 by Don Ignacio González Vargas at his Fabrica el Centenario, Siete Leguas is named in honour of the Mexican Revolutionary Pancho Villa's favourite horse, which served

S

him throughout the revolution. The distillery, now called Tequila Siete Leguas (NOM 1120), uses brick ovens to cook its mostly estate-grown blue agave. Then a portion of the piñas are crushed using a tahona while another portion is pressed using a roller mill. The must is naturally fermented with the fibres before being double distilled in small copper pot stills. The blanco is bottled unaged, the reposado is aged for eight months in white oak barrels, the añejo is matured for twenty-four months, the extra añejo for five years and the Siete Leguas Single Barrel selects from barrels aged between five and ten years. Besides producing high-quality tequila, Siete Leguas gained notoriety for being the original source for Patrón Tequila before Patrón built its own distillery.

Silver

See "Blanco" (page 43).

Simple syrup

See "Sugar syrup" (page 217).

Songs about tequila | HISTORY

SEE ALSO
Tequila Sunrise p233

Since at least the 1950s, tequila has been a recurring theme in pop, country, hip-hop and dance music. One of the first examples was 1957's "Drinking Tequila" by Jim Reeves, a country song about a cowboy drinking in Juárez, Mexico. One year later, the iconic instrumental "Tequila" by the Champs earned a gold disc. Then, in 1977, Jimmy Buffett released his iconic "Margaritaville", which peaked at Number 8 on the USA Billboard Hot 100. Since then, tequila has been mentioned or featured in songs by such disparate artists as the Eagles, Sammy Hagar, Joe Nichols, Kenny Chesney, Alanis Morrissette, Cypress Hill and Paradiso Girls. The common thread of these songs depicts tequila as a party spirit that causes people to overindulge, use poor judgment and act abnormally from their usual self. This is an unfortunate stereotype that puts the blame for people's poor choices about alcohol consumption on what can be a meticulously crafted and beautiful spirit.

Sonora | REGION

Located in the north-west corner of Mexico, Sonora is divided north–south into three sections: the Gulf of California in the west, rolling plains in the centre of the state and the Sierra Madre Occidental mountains in the east. The state is primarily made up of arid or semiarid grasslands and deserts. The economy and culture of Sonora has been dominated by ranching and the idealized figure of the vaquero (cowboy). Mining, farming, fishing and tourism make up the other major industries. Like many other parts of Mexico, agave and distilled spirits produced from agave have been important to the culture and traditions of the state. In the centre of Sonora, the town of Bacanora became famous for a spirit made in a very similar way to mezcal, but the Sonoran spirit took its name from the town. Bacanora received a Denomination of Origin (DO) in 2000 and is almost identical to mezcal. However, one interesting difference is that any age statement on the bottle can be given as a weighted average of the volume of each component, instead of the age of the youngest spirit in the bottle.

SEE ALSO
Bacanora *p35*
Denomination of Origin for
  Bacanora (DOB)*p79*

SEE ALSO
Denomination of Origin for
Sotol (DOS) *p80*

Sotol | CLASSIFICATION

A distilled spirit made from a spieces of dasylirion (*D. wheeleri*), also known as the desert spoon or common sotol. In pre-Columbian times, the indigenous peoples used the desert-spoon fibres for weaving and cooked the piñas and ate them like giant artichokes. While the desert spoon grows from the American Southwest to southern Mexico, most sotol production has historically been centred in the deserts and mountains of the Mexican state of Chihuahua. During US Prohibition, Chihuahua was producing around 300,000 litres (over 79,000gal [US]) of sotol each year, some of which was crossing over the border into Texas. The Mexican government began cracking down on the production of sotol both to promote consumption of other Mexican spirits and to maintain good relations with the USA. Finally, in the 1990s, Mexico issued the first-ever permit for the legal production of sotol and, in 2002, sotol received its own Denomination of Origin (DO) covering production in the states of Coahuila, Chihuahua and Durango. However, the recognition of sotol's DO has not been included in any trade agreements with the USA so, at the time of writing, there are two Texas distilleries making a USA sotol from local varieties of dasylirion.

SEE ALSO
Glycerine *p113*

Sugar syrup | ADDITIVE

Also known as simple syrup, sugar syrup is commonly used to sweeten beverages and cocktails because of its ability to integrate into a drink more easily than granulated sugar. Often made with a 1:1 ratio of refined cane sugar and water, sugar syrup is made by gently stirring sugar and warm water until the sugar is fully dissolved. Sugar syrup can also be made with higher concentrations of sugar to water, such as 2:1 or even 5:1. According to Mexican regulations, sugar syrup may be added to all categories of tequila, except for blanco tequila, as a mellowing agent to soften the flavour of tequila. Like salt added to food, sugar syrup added to tequila can both enhance the desirable flavours of the spirits and soften the sensation of the alcohol on the palate.

Tahona | PRODUCTION

A very heavy stone or concrete wheel used to crush cooked agave in an Egyptian mill. Before the advent of mechanical shredders or diffusers, the tahona was an advance in tequila and mezcal production that utilized labour from a mule or horse to pull the tahona around its axis in the mill. Before the tahona, cooked agave would be crushed by hand in a hollowed-out log called a canoa (canoe) with a large wooden mallet. Today, tahonas are used in both traditional tequila and mezcal production and are one indicator of potential quality.

Tails (*colas*) | PRODUCTION

A mixture of chemical compounds that have a higher boiling point than ethanol. During distillation, after most alcohol has distilled out, heavier chemicals such as butanol, fusel alcohols (also known as fusel oils), acetic acid (vinegar) and furfural come off the still. The term "fusel" comes from the German word for "bad liquor". Fusels have an oily texture and produce a harsh burning sensation in the mouth and throat when left in spirits. When spirits have a significant burn (a sign of low quality), it usually means that the distiller has allowed too many tails into the hearts cut. Furfural is a known carcinogen, and

its presence in food and beverages is regulated by many countries, including Mexico. Tequila is allowed to have no more than 4mg per 100ml of spirit while mezcal is allowed to have no more than 5mg per 100ml.

Tamaulipas | REGION

SEE ALSO
Denomination of Origin for
  Tequila (DOT) p83
Normas Oficiales Mexicanas
  (NOM) p171

While most tequila-producing states are in the central and western regions of Mexico, Tamaulipas is in the north-east, in a region bordering Texas and the Gulf of Mexico. After the Mexican–American War of 1846–8, Tamaulipas lost about 25 percent of its total area in the Treaty of Guadalupe Hidalgo. The geography of the region splits into two: the eastern portion is mostly made of coastal plains, while the western portion is dominated by the Sierra Madre Oriental, with peaks rising to 3,280m (10,760ft) above sea level. The economy of the northern portion is dominated by trade with Texas, while the economy of the southern portion is shaped by the petrochemical industry. Since the Denomination of Origin for Tequila (DOT) in 1977, 11 of Tamaulipas's southernmost municipalities have been allowed to grow blue agave for tequila and produce tequila. At the time of writing, most of the agave grown in Tamaulipas is sold to distilleries outside the state, with only two currently operating in the state itself: Tequilera la Gonzaleña (NOM 1127) and Tequilera 8 Mesas (NOM 1587).

Tapatio | BRAND

SEE ALSO
Beam Suntory p40
Familia Camarena p107
Normas Oficiales Mexicanas
  (NOM) p171

In 1937, Don Felipe Camarena founded the La Alteña distillery after finding success growing and selling agaves. The company has remained in the family, and today the rechristened Tequila

Tapatio distillery (NOM 1139) is operated by Don Felipe's grandchildren: Lilianna, Gabriela and Carlos. As head distiller, Carlos Camarena oversees the entire production process, during which the piñas are cooked in brick ovens then pressed in a roller mill, and the cooked agave juice is fermented and double distilled in copper pot stills. The mystique of Tapatio Tequila was enhanced by the fact that for many years it was not exported out of Mexico, and its reputation now seems credible since the Camarenas began making Beam Suntory's El Tesoro Tequila. However, today, the company bottles five expressions of Tapatio for export: two unaged blancos, one bottled at 40% ABV and the second at 55% ABV; the reposado, which is matured for four to six months in used bourbon barrels; the añejo, aged for eighteen months; and the Excelencia Extra Añejo, which is aged in new charred American oak barrels for four years.

Tequila | CLASSIFICATION

A spirit named after the Mexican town of Tequila in the Tequila Valley. Mexican regulations define tequila as a regional distilled beverage produced from *Agave tequilana* var. azul. The agave sugars in the piñas must be hydrolysed with or without cooking and fermented with wild or cultivated yeast. Tequila fermentations may be enriched by adding up to 49 percent of the total sugars from other non-agave sources before distillation, but they cannot be mixed with other non-tequila spirits post-distillation. Post-distillation tequila may be matured in oak barrels and can have added colouring, flavouring and sweeteners. While agave spirits have been made in Jalisco since at least the mid-1500s, author Ian Chadwick argues that the drink we

know as tequila did not really come into existence until the late 19th century when distillers began to use of above-ground brick ovens that cooked the piñas with indirect heat. This is also when distillers such as Sauza and Cuervo began to refer to their spirits as mezcal de tequila, before it was shortened to tequila. In 1949, Mexico passed the first laws regulating where and how tequila could be made, which was followed in 1974 with the first Denomination of Origin (DO) that would help protect tequila outside of Mexico.

Tequila Arette | BRAND

SEE ALSO
Hearts *p126*
Normas Oficiales Mexicanas
  (NOM) *p171*

Created in 1986 by Eduardo and Jaime Orendain to celebrate the two gold medals that General Humberto Mariles and his horse won during the 1948 London Olympics. The Orendain family has been distilling in the Tequila Valley since 1900 when Don Eduardo Orendain opened El Llano (today Tequila Arette de Jalisco NOM 1109). The Orendains produce three lines of Arette tequilas: Clásica, Artesanal and Unique. The Clásica line starts with piñas cooked in an autoclave, pressed with a roller mill, fermented in stainless-steel tanks and double distilled in stainless-steel pot stills with copper coils. The Artesanal line starts with agaves that are slightly more mature cooked and pressed in the same way; however, the must is fermented in concrete tanks, which are cooler and produce a slower fermentation. During distillation, a narrower hearts cut is taken compared with the Clásica, and the aged expressions are matured twice as long.

Tequila Cabrito | BRAND

SEE ALSO
100 percent agave *p13*
Mixto *p163*
Normas Oficiales Mexicanas
  (NOM) *p171*

One of the bestselling tequilas in Mexico, Tequila Cabrito was founded in 1904 by Don

Pepe Centinela and is made at Tequila Centinela (NOM 1140) in the southern Los Altos. In Mexico, Cabrito is a mixto tequila bottled at 38% ABV, while the version exported to the USA is made from 100 percent agave and bottled at 40% ABV. The agaves are cooked in brick ovens, fermented in steel tanks and distilled once in a stainless-steel pot still, and then distilled a second time in a copper pot still. Cabrito Silver tequila is bottled unaged, while the Cabrito Reposado is matured for two months in oak barrels before bottling.

Tequila Daisy | COCKTAIL

SEE ALSO
Margarita *p149*
Picador *p189*
Tequila Sour *p231*

Recorded by Jerry Thomas in his 1887 book *The Bar-Tender's Guide,* Tequila Daisies are traditionally tall drinks that combine spirit, sweetener, citrus and soda water. However, today, many Daisies are made up in a spirit-forward variation. And, while it is not known when the Tequila Daisy first appeared, the versatility of the drink and agave spirits proved to be well matched.

TEQUILA DAISY RECIPE

15ML / ½FL OZ LEMON JUICE
½ TSP CASTER/SUPERFINE SUGAR
60ML / 2FL OZ REPOSADO TEQUILA
15ML / ½FL OZ ORANGE LIQUEUR (E.G. GRAND MARNIER)
SODA WATER

Stir the lemon juice and sugar in a cocktail shaker until the sugar is dissolved. Add the tequila, orange liqueur and fill with ice. Shake until cold and strain into a chilled cocktail glass and top with a splash of soda water.

T
227

Tequila Fortaleza | BRAND

SEE ALSO
Normas Oficiales Mexicanas (NOM) *p171*
Sauza Tequila *p211*
Tahona *p219*

In 2005, Guillermo Erickson Sauza, great-great grandson of Cenobio Sauza launched Tequila

Fortaleza, continuing his family's century-long legacy of distilling tequila. Sometime around 1946, when Francisco Javier Sauza inherited the Sauza company, he purchased an estate to grow agave and built a hacienda and a small distillery that he called La Constancia. In 1968, Francisco shut the distillery because of its inefficient and small production and turned it into a museum. However, when Francisco sold the Sauza company in 1976, the family retained the small estate distillery. In 1999, Guillermo began the process of refurbishing the distillery, now called Tequila Los Abuelos (NOM 1493), and set about making traditional tequila using brick ovens, a tahona, wooden fermentation vats and copper pot stills.

SEE ALSO
Brown-Forman *p49*
Cristalino *p73*
El Jimador *p99*
Normas Oficiales Mexicanas
  (NOM) *p171*

Tequila Herradura | BRAND

In 1870, Félix López founded Hacienda San José del Refugio, which grew blue agave and produced tequila. In the early 1900s, López's son Aurelio renamed the company and tequila Herradura (horseshoe), believing it would bring good luck. The company remained family-run for over a century, until 2007, when Brown-Forman purchased Herradura and all its assets for $776 million, and the distillery was officially renamed Brown-Forman Tequila Mexico (NOM 1119). Herradura has always produced 100 percent agave tequilas made by cooking piñas in brick ovens, pressing them with roller mills, fermenting the cooked agave juice and double distilling in large stainless-steel pot stills. All of the tequilas are aged in used American whiskey barrels and bottled at 40% ABV. The silver tequila is rested for 45 days, the reposado is matured for 11 months, the añejo is aged for 2 years, the extra añejo is aged just over 4 years

and Herradura Ultra is a blend of añejo and extra-añejo tequilas that is then carbon-filtered to remove the colour.

Tequila Ocho | BRAND

SEE ALSO
Normas Oficiales Mexicanas (NOM) p171
Tapatio p221

A company created in 2008 as a partnership between Carlos Camarena and Tomas Estes to explore what roll terroir plays in the flavour profile of tequila. While a number of tequilas bill themselves as estate tequilas, the Camarena family has about 50 separate plantations spread throughout Los Altos de Jalisco. For each bottling, Estes and Camarena take ripe agave from one ranch only, and cook, mill, ferment and distil that one harvest into single-estate tequilas never seen before. At their distillery Cía. Tequilera Los Alambiques (NOM 1474), the piñas are cooked in brick ovens, pressed with a roller mill and fermented without fibres in open wooden tanks. The fermented must is first stripped in a large stainless-steel pot still and then distilled a second time in a copper pot still. All the tequilas are bottled at 40% ABV: the plata is unaged, the reposado is rested for eight months, the añejo is aged for one year and the extra añejo is matured for three years in ex-American whiskey barrels.

Tequila Regulatory Council

See "Consejo Regulador del Tequila" (page 71).

Tequila Sour | COCKTAIL

SEE ALSO
Margarita p149
Picador p189
Tequila Daisy p227

Like the Daisy, the Sour is a classic group of cocktails recorded by famed barman Jerry Thomas. The Sour is a mix of spirit, citrus and sweetener. Sours are interesting because of their

variety: some are served up in a stemmed Sour glass, and some in a Old Fashioned glass; some come with a fruit-salad garnish and some with an egg-white foam. This variation has perpetuated the drink's popularity for over 100 years.

TEQUILA SOUR RECIPE

60ML / 2FL OZ TEQUILA (BLANCO OR REPOSADO)
25ML / ¾FL OZ LEMON JUICE
25ML / ¾FL OZ SIMPLE SYRUP
LEMON WHEEL
MARASCHINO CHERRY

Fill a cocktail shaker with ice and add the tequila, lemon juice and syrup. Shake until cold and strain into a chilled Sour or other stemmed cocktail glass. Garnish with a lemon slice on the rim and a maraschino cherry. For an egg-white version, add tequila, lemon juice, syrup and 1 egg white into a shaker and shake vigorously. Add ice and give a second shake to chill the drink. Double strain into a Sour glass or an Old Fashioned glass and garnish the foam with an aromatic cocktail bitter such as mole bitters.

SEE ALSO
Tequila Daisy *p227*

Tequila Sunrise | COCKTAIL

A tequila-centric tall drink with two origin stories and two recipes. The "original" Tequila Sunrise was created by Gene Sulit at the Arizona Biltmore Hotel in Phoenix, Arizona, sometime in the 1930s. This version of the drink called for tequila, crème de cassis, lime juice and soda water. Fast-forward about 40 years and the "modern" Tequila Sunrise was created by Bobby Lazoff and Billy Rice while working The Trident restaurant in Sausalito, California. Their version was a combination of tequila, orange juice and grenadine syrup. Legend has it that, in 1972, concert promoter Bill Graham threw a private party at The Trident to mark the start of the Rolling Stones' world tour. There, the Stones fell in love with the modern Tequila Sunrise and the drink's presence and popularity spread

T
233

across the USA like wildfire. A year later, Jose Cuervo began listing the cocktail on the back of its bottles and the Eagles named the first single off their album *Desperado* (1973) after the drink.

ORIGINAL TEQUILA SUNRISE RECIPE

45ML / 1½FL OZ TEQUILA (BLANCO OR REPOSADO)
JUICE FROM ½ LIME
120ML / 4FL OZ SODA WATER
25 ML / ¾FL OZ CRÈME DE CASSIS
LIME WHEEL
MARASCHINO CHERRY

Fill a chilled Collins glass with ice and add tequila, lime juice and soda water, leaving the glass a little less than full. Slowly add the crème de cassis, allowing it to drop to the bottom of the glass, and garnish with a lime wheel and a maraschino cherry.

MODERN TEQUILA SUNRISE RECIPE

45ML / 1½FL OZ TEQUILA (BLANCO OR REPOSADO)
120ML / 4FL OZ ORANGE JUICE
15ML / ½FL OZ GRENADINE
ORANGE WHEEL
RED COCKTAIL CHERRY

Fill a chilled Collins glass with ice and add the tequila and orange juice. Slowly pour the grenadine around the inside edge of the glass, allowing it to sink to the bottom. Garnish with an orange wheel and a bright-red cocktail cherry, for the true 1970s feel.

Tequila Valley | REGION

SEE ALSO
Altos de Jalisco *p26*
Jalisco *p137*

The largest tequila-producing region in Mexico, the Tequila Valley extends from Guadalajara in Jalisco, north-west to the border with Nayarit. The Tequila Valley sits at about 1,180m (about 3,870ft) in elevation and in the shadow of the 2,920m (9,580ft) Volcán de Tequila, a stratovolcano similar to Mount Fuji or Mount St Helens that last erupted around 220,000 years ago. Because of the volcano, the valley floor is covered in rich volcanic soil, which is very high in nutrients. The quality of the soil combined

with the generally warmer climate compared to Los Altos allows agaves grown in the valley to mature slightly faster than those from the highlands. Tequilas produced from lowland agaves are described as tasting earthier and with more pepper. However, when a panel of experts blind-tasted tequila from Los Altos and the Tequila Valley, the region played no role in their preferences for the majority of tasters. Fortaleza, Casa Noble and Jose Cuervo are among the well-known tequilas produced in the Tequila Valley.

Triple sec | COCKTAIL INGREDIENT

An orange-flavoured liqueur commonly used in cocktails to add flavour and sweetness to the drink. Triple sec refers to the fact that the orange-flavoured spirit was traditionally distilled three times before the addition of sugar, and the name has become a generic term for liqueurs flavoured with dried bitter and/or sweet orange peels. Triple sec first appeared around the middle of the 19th century and was sometimes referred to as curaçao triple sec, indicating it was a triple-distilled liqueur that used laraha citrus peel. However, Cointreau, a popular brand-name triple sec, is not technically a curaçao because it does not use laraha citrus as a flavouring. In practice, this means that curaçao, Cointreau and triple sec are all interchangeable in cocktails but they each have a slightly different flavour and price point, with triple sec often being the most economical.

T

237

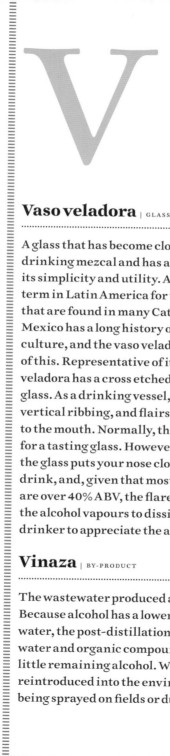

V

Vaso veladora | GLASSWARE

A glass that has become closely associated with drinking mezcal and has a certain elegance in its simplicity and utility. A veladora is a Spanish term in Latin America for the prayer candles that are found in many Catholic churches. Mexico has a long history of mixing religion and culture, and the vaso veladora is a great example of this. Representative of its former use, the vaso veladora has a cross etched into the bottom of the glass. As a drinking vessel, it is a short glass with vertical ribbing, and flairs slightly from the base to the mouth. Normally, this is not a good design for a tasting glass. However, the short stature of the glass puts your nose close to the fill level of the drink, and, given that most traditional mezcals are over 40% ABV, the flared mouth allows the alcohol vapours to dissipate, enabling the drinker to appreciate the aroma of the spirit.

Vinaza | BY-PRODUCT

V

239

The wastewater produced after distillation. Because alcohol has a lower boiling point than water, the post-distillation mixture of residual water and organic compounds have very little remaining alcohol. When the vinaza is reintroduced into the environment, either by being sprayed on fields or dumped into a pond or stream, it absorbs oxygen from the environment, decreasing the amount of oxygen in the water or the soil. This is referred to as biochemical oxygen demand (BOD). Oxygen is needed to breakdown organic materials in the vinaza as well as other organic material in the soil. If the vinaza is dumped into a stream, the BOD can create dead zones where no fish or aquatic plant life can live because of the lack of oxygen. Historically, when mezcal was just a local commodity used for ceremonies and celebrations, the amount of vinaza generated was small enough for the environment to absorb. However, now that mezcal has entered the world market and production has increased by over 1,000 percent, vinaza, especially in areas with lots of distillers, poses a significant environmental challenge.

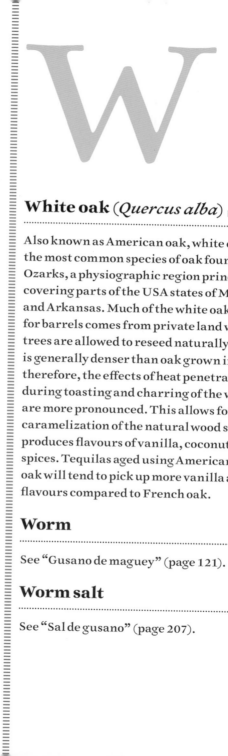

White oak (*Quercus alba*) | PLANT

Also known as American oak, white oak is
the most common species of oak found in the
Ozarks, a physiographic region principally
covering parts of the USA states of Missouri
and Arkansas. Much of the white oak harvested
for barrels comes from private land where the
trees are allowed to reseed naturally. White oak
is generally denser than oak grown in Europe;
therefore, the effects of heat penetration
during toasting and charring of the wood
are more pronounced. This allows for more
caramelization of the natural wood sugars and
produces flavours of vanilla, coconut and baking
spices. Tequilas aged using American white
oak will tend to pick up more vanilla and wood
flavours compared to French oak.

Worm

See "Gusano de maguey" (page 121).

Worm salt

See "Sal de gusano" (page 207).

Xylose | PLANT

A wood sugar that derives its name from the Greek word for wood (*xylon*). Xylose is a monosaccharide that can be produced from the breakdown of hemicellulose, present in almost all plant cell walls, including oak. When oak is formed into barrels, the inside is usually toasted from the heat used to bend the wood. During this heating process, hemicellulose is degraded, releasing xylose. When alcohol such as wine or tequila is put into the barrels, the spirit further degrades the wood, causing a small release of xylose into the drink, which can add a slight sweetness.

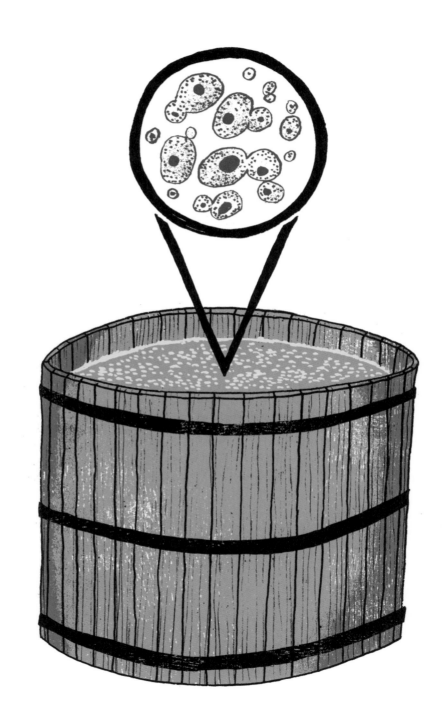

Yeast | PRODUCTION

A single-cell organism that is part of the fungus family, yeast has existed on Earth for about 150 million years and evolved by feeding off sugars in pine sap. Even though the Egyptians were making beer over 5,000 years ago, humans did not understand what yeast did until 1857, when French microbiologist Louis Pasteur proved that it was responsible for the conversion of sugar into alcohol. Before people understood how to propagate yeast to ferment, they would either allow wild yeast to ferment the must naturally or add a portion of a previous ferment including live yeast into a new batch of must. Through a process of selective pressure by humans, yeast has multiplied into 1,500 varieties that can produce different flavours and different amounts of alcohol, and some more suited for CO_2 production are used for making bread. Today, most tequila is made using cultivated yeast, although many ancestral and artisanal mezcals are still produced using wild yeast to ferment their musts.

Zacatecas | REGION

Located in north-central Mexico, Zacatecas is
best known for its silver and mineral deposits
as well as its important role in the Mexican
Revolution (*c.* 1910–20). The state has an average
elevation of 2,230m (7,361ft), with a central high
plateau surrounded by mountain ranges in the
east and the west. In general, Zacatecas has a
cool, dry climate, and receives most of its rainfall
between June and September. Because of this,
less than 15 percent of the state is able to support
agriculture, though large portions are well
suited for grazing, which is fitting because the
state's name comes from the Nahuatl phrase for
"where there is abundant grass". Zacatecas also
has a long tradition of growing agave and, since
colonial times, of making mezcal. In 1994, when
mezcal received its Denomination of Origin
(DO), Zacatecas was one of the original states
included in the DO. One of the largest producers
of mezcal in Zacatecas is Real de Jalpa, which
makes joven, reposado and añejo mezcal under a
few different brand names.

Index

page numbers in *italic* refer to illustrations

Acknowledgments

I would like to take a moment to thank those who made this book possible. First, I would like to thank Joe Cottington of Octopus Publishing Group for approaching me with this project and continuing our productive working relationship. I would also like to thank the rest of the team at Octopus for editing and illustrating my words into a beautiful book. Thank you to Mike Morales, Lisa Pietsch, Susan Coss, Max Garrone and Ana Valenzuela for welcoming me further into the world of agave spirits. Thanks also goes to David T. Smith and Bill Owens for helping me grow as a writer and spirits professional, and to Greg Hatfield and Matthew White for sharing a couple of very special glasses of tequila with me. In addition, I want to thank the farmers, field workers, distillers and producers who dedicate themselves to making fantastic spirits from the noble agave. Thank you to Graciela Angeles Carreño, Antonio Carlos Martinez, Edna Gpe Viveros, Marco Ochoa, Ulises Torrentera, Sandra Ortiz Brena, Sten Maldonado, Leticia Hernandez Galguera, Doug French and Jason Paul Cox for sharing your time, knowledge and passion for mezcal with me.

Lastly, I want to thank my wife Tia and our two sons Giorgio and Elio. Thank you for giving me the time and support to write, without which my work would be in vain.

For my wife, Tia.

An Hachette UK Company

www.hachette.co.uk

First published in Great Britain in 2019 by Mitchell Beazley,
an imprint of Octopus Publishing Group Ltd
Carmelite House
50 Victoria Embankment
London EC4Y 0DZ
www.octopusbooks.co.uk
www.octopusbooksusa.com

Design and Layout Copyright © Octopus Publishing Group Ltd 2019
Text Copyright © Eric Zandona 2019
Illustration © Tom Jay 2019

Distributed in the US by
Hachette Book Group
1290 Avenue of the Americas
4th and 5th Floors
New York, NY 10104

Distributed in Canada by
Canadian Manda Group
664 Annette St.
Toronto, Ontario, Canada M6S 2C8

ISBN 978-1-78472-547-1

A CIP catalogue record for this book is available from the British Library.

Printed and bound in China

10 9 8 7 6 5 4 3 2 1

Commissioning Editor: Joe Cottington
Creative Director: Jonathan Christie
Illustrator: Tom Jay
Junior Editor: Sarah Vaughan
Copy Editor: Robert Tuesley Anderson
Senior Production Controller: Allison Gonsalves

About the author

A native of the San Francisco Bay Area, Eric Zandona is Director of Spirits Information at the American Distilling Institute, and a writer for *Distiller* magazine. He also runs the website EZdrinking.com and is an author/editor for the ADI's publishing arm, White Mule Press. In 2017, Eric began a year-long residency in Oaxaca drinking and learning about Mexican gin, rum, whiskey and agave spirits. Today, he and his family live in Vancouver, Washington.